SONORAN DESERT SUMMER

JOHN ALCOCK

Sonoran Desert Summer

Illustrated by Marilyn Hoff Stewart

THE UNIVERSITY OF ARIZONA PRESS   TUCSON

The University of Arizona Press
Copyright © 1990
The Arizona Board of Regents
All Rights Reserved

This book was set in 9½-point Esprit.
♾ This book is printed on acid-free, archival-quality paper.
Manufactured in the United States of America.

94 93 92 91 90 5 4 3 2 1

LIBRARY OF CONGRESS CATALOGING-IN-PUBLICATION DATA
Alcock, John, 1942–
    Sonoran desert summer / John Alcock ; illustrated by Marilyn Hoff
Stewart.
        p.   cm.
    Includes bibliographical references.
    ISBN 0-8165-1150-0 (alk. paper)
        1. Desert ecology — Sonoran Desert.   2. Summer — Sonoran Desert.
    3. Sonoran Desert. I. Title.
    QH104.5.S58A42   1990   89-20235
    574.5'2652'0979173 — dc20   CIP

British Library Cataloguing in Publication data are available.

Original drawings copyright © 1989 by Marilyn Hoff Stewart

Contents

Illustrations

Preface

The Sonoran Desert of southern Arizona and northwestern Mexico is a wonderful place for a biologist to live, even if the weather sometimes makes us forget just how delightful the desert really is. Ironically, it is the extreme hostility of the climate that is responsible for the exotic and intriguing nature of the desert's biology. Only very special plants and animals can survive and reproduce in a place that may receive as little as six inches of rain in a year, a place where the temperature may rise above one hundred degrees each day for months on end.

Learning how Sonoran Desert plants and animals cope with their off-the-scale environment provides me with both pleasure and a livelihood; I teach at Arizona State University in Tempe, near the northern edge of the range of the saguaro cactus. Part of a professor's job is to be a researcher, and I have chosen to investigate the ways in which males of certain desert insects locate mates. My esoteric studies are tolerated, even encouraged, by my university. As a result I am able to spend many hours outdoors, wandering about a little mountain in the Tonto National Forest within an hour's drive of Greater Phoenix.

This book has been inspired largely by the animals and plants that I have come to know and admire in the course of my research on Usery Mountain. In the chapters that follow I report some things I have discovered about desert biology. I also describe the findings of other biologists who have explored life in the Sonoran Desert. I hope I can convey to you my appreciation and enthusiasm for the organisms that have evolved in this severe and beautiful place.

Writing a book is a cooperative enterprise that involves many helpful collaborators. I would like to acknowledge first the other biologists whose research enabled me to learn more about the desert, with special thanks to colleagues and students at Arizona State University, among them Steve Goldsmith, Stuart Fisher, Neil Hadley, Therese Markow, Ron Rutowski, Christopher Thompson, and Glenn Walsberg.

I also am grateful to Susan E. Abrams for her encouragement and exceedingly sound editorial advice. At the University of Arizona Press I have been lucky to have a fine editor and helpful reviewers of the manuscript, among them Paul Martin. I am very fortunate that Marilyn Hoff Stewart agreed to illustrate the book with her accurate and appealing drawings.

Two of the chapters in this book first appeared, in slightly different form, in *Natural History* and *Pacific Discovery* magazines. I thank the editors of each for permission to reprint this material here.

Finally, I thank my wife Sue and sons Joe and Nick for sharing their lives with me in the Sonoran Desert of Arizona.

SONORAN DESERT SUMMER

May

A loggerhead shrike drops down the hillside, a stroboscopic flicker of blacks and whites on the sunburnt desert vegetation. It has not rained for six weeks, except for one brief and now barely remembered shower in mid-April.

The sun shares a cloudless sky with what appears to be a heat-crazed turkey vulture; the bird loops slowly back and forth in a seemingly aimless pattern, moving but going nowhere.

It will be 107 degrees by midafternoon. Summer has begun to assert itself in the Sonoran Desert of central Arizona.

The vulture drifts along the ridgeline, its black wings catching the heated air that pushes up shimmering from the baked gravel of the desert floor. The bird's naked red head turns and one eye looks down on a landscape that appears to be slowly contracting as it patiently, numbly waits for rain. The rush of air over the vulture's long wings produces a faint, breathy whistle that may be a sigh of resignation. Or a whisper of acceptance.

The Fall and Decline of a Giant

The vultures that criss-cross the desert to the west of the Usery Mountains look down upon an immense corpse pressed against the ground, but the sight of the dead saguaro cactus probably sends no shivers of delight through these observers. All that remains of the moribund saguaro at the start of another summer is a nearly naked skeleton, but it was once the biggest living thing for miles around, a true giant whose life ended in a wild August windstorm almost four years ago. It was the monsoon season then, and moist air drawn up from a tropical storm in the Gulf of California had fueled a series of spectacular late afternoon thunderstorms. With the ground softened and the saguaro heavy with stored water, a violent wind swept across the desert toppling one large saguaro after another. When the giant saguaro's trunk fractured at its base, thirty-five feet of cactus, tons of trunk, thirty massive arms, a vacant Harris's hawk nest, and part of a neighboring ironwood tree slammed into the wet desert soil.

After the storm, unaware of the disaster, I went looking for the giant to admire again its magnificent symmetry and design. When I failed to see its upraised arms looming over the desert flatland I thought perhaps I had lost my way. I found the cactus soon enough, however, lying on the ground, its green arms stretched out pointing to the south. In my unhappiness I initially attempted to pin the blame for this misfortune on my fellow Phoenicians, thinking that perhaps someone had chopped down the cactus in the kind of exuberant nihilism favored by desert vandals. But there was no evidence of axework anywhere, and in looking about I discovered other fallen saguaros in the neighborhood, each body laid out neatly in a north-south orientation.

A random sample of twelve wind-blown saguaros (not including the fallen giant) showed an average of 5.3 arms apiece among the victims, whereas the nearest still-standing specimens averaged just 1.0 arm each. Although many fat arms afford more space for flowers, this reproductive benefit is purchased at the price of top-heaviness, which increases a saguaro's risk of death in a windstorm.

Even after its fall I continued to visit the giant saguaro to record its reunion with the desert soil. Although the cactus was no longer alive, it continued for some time to serve a community of desert organisms that replaced the gila woodpeckers and Harris's hawks, the white-winged doves and curve-billed thrashers that had occupied and used the saguaro while it was alive.

Within two months of its collapse the giant saguaro began to deliquesce as bacteria, *Erwinia carnegieana*, took full advantage of the many entry points created by the fracture of the trunk and arms to attack the soft internal parts of the plant. From rips and tears fluids seeped down the pleated body of the cactus, coating its surface with a shiny brown lacquer.

Saguaro-rotting bacteria possess the enzyme cellulase, and so they can consume the cell walls of cacti. As the cells disintegrate, their contents become accessible to other microbes, including certain yeasts and molds, that join the bacteria in a race to convert macro-saguaros into their microscopic descendants.

The metabolic by-products of the various microorganisms create a rich organic soup of alcohols, acetates, and the like that arise from the fermentation of glucose once contained in the plant's cells. Among these materials are volatiles that attract both scavenging cactophilic flies and human researchers, who follow their noses to the not unpleasant odor of rotting cacti in search of the specialized insect fauna associated with these plants.

The persons most adept at sniffing out cactus rots are *Drosophila* geneticists who have studied the fruit flies that reproduce at these sites. William Heed and his colleagues at the University of Arizona have discovered that the Sonoran Desert possesses its own specialized stable of *Drosophila* species, each of which tends to be associated with a particular species of cactus. Thus *Drosophila pachea* exploits rot pockets in senita cactus, whereas *Drosophila mojavensis* breeds almost exclusively in agria and organ pipe cacti. *Drosophila nigrospiracula* occurs only on saguaro and cardon.

Heed and his coworkers have linked the specificity of Sonoran Desert *Drosophila* to the defensive chemistry of their cacti hosts. The columnar succulent cacti that feed desert fruit flies manufacture chemical substances designed to deter potential consumers. Senita produces high concentrations of toxic alkaloids; agrias and organ pipes turn out very different but equally potent deterrents in the form of triterpene glycosides. In order to feed on decaying senita a fruit fly requires specialized enzymes that can deal with senita alkaloids, whereas a different metabolism altogether is called for to cope with agria's defensive triterpene glycosides. The diverse chemical challenges offered by the different desert cacti have, so the argument goes, favored the specialization exhibited by Sonoran Desert fruit flies.

The cosmopolitan kitchen fruit fly and favorite of laboratory geneticists, *Drosophila melanogaster*, on the other hand, is able to live around the world because it avoids decaying plant material with special toxic compounds in favor of the edible fruits of many chemically nondistinctive species of plants.

As a saguaro begins to fall apart, one of the first insect colonizers to arrive is *Drosophila nigrospiracula*. Saguaros, like senitas, employ alkaloids as chemical defenders in their cells, and the saguaro fruit fly has evolved the metabolic equipment that enables it to deal with the special alkaloids present in the dead tissues of rotting saguaros. The fly cannot survive on tissues that contain senita alkaloids or that contain organ pipe triterpene glycosides.

In and along the rivulets of exudate, fruit flies assemble to feed and mate. Females with clutches of mature eggs leave the oozes to visit males, which set up mating territories nearby on the cracked skin of the saguaro. Each male maintains a circular arena, two to three inches across, from which he repels intruder males while welcoming incoming females with a complex courtship display.

Therese Markow of Arizona State University has watched some females move from one male to the next, apparently evaluating the courtship performance of several individuals before finally settling on a mate. After copulating, females enter tiny crevices in the cactus that provide access to pockets of saguaro flesh in the early phases of decay. Here they oviposit, laying eggs that hatch into minute grubs. The larvae find themselves surrounded by a food that they, like their parents, can digest, thanks to enzymes that defuse the alkaloid "bombs" in saguaro tissues.

Saguaro fruit flies are not the only flies to take advantage of the mountain of food in decaying saguaros. The cactus fly, *Odontoloxozus longicornis*, also comes to feed and mate near necrotic saguaro tissues. Although the fruit fly is an ordinary-looking creature, the cactus fly appears to be the invention of an out-of-work science fiction writer. On legs that seem much too long for their slender bodies, the red-eyed flies scuttle about the surface of the saguaro, sipping fluid exudate and darting at each other.

Lee Olsen and Raymond Ruckman report that cactus flies "continually engage in amorous antics." This is particularly true when groups form in the shelter of a cranny in a decaying saguaro; here males indulge in a race to contact, court and mate with as many females as possible – with about forty percent of all encounters ending in copulation.

But not all males employ the same tactics. Some individuals move out into the open to find and defend fine cracks in saguaro skin above well-decayed but still firm rot pockets. These are the oviposition sites used by females; by monopolizing such a location a male *always* is accepted by a female just before she lays her eggs in his territory. While she inserts her slender abdomen into the crack to oviposit, the male stands guard, ready to use his long legs to repel male intruders that attempt to steal and mate with his partner.

Because the food requirements of cactus fly larvae consist of well-rotted saguaro tissues, this species generally arrives at fallen saguaros after the first fruit flies. A still later colonist is a hover fly, *Volucella isabellina*, a large, orange-bodied insect that lives up to its name by hovering noisily in the air as if suspended on a string. Gravid females do not come to a saguaro until part of it has decayed into a pool of liquid exudate.

When conditions are ripe, a female hangs upside down from cactus spines, to which she attaches a cluster of eggs; when the first-instar larvae emerge they somehow manage to wriggle their way to a puddle of fermenting juices under a fallen limb or within a still-standing saguaro. In they go to drink their way to maturity.

Because such pools contain a considerable amount of alcohol, hover fly larvae have evolved an astounding insensitivity to high concentrations of alcohol. Timothy Myles at the University of Arizona placed four mature larvae in seventy percent ethanol, thinking to pickle the grubs as museum specimens. Although the procedure works smoothly for the vast majority of insects, the hover fly larvae were still very much alive ninety minutes later.

Thus, over time, a fallen saguaro offers many changing environments, which are exploited in turn by bacteria, yeasts, fruit flies, cactus flies and hover flies, to say nothing of an army of other scavengers and predators of scavengers.

The giant saguaro in my habitual hiking area played host to all these creatures. Because of unequal rates of decay at various limbs, a complete community of saguaro rot specialists coexisted at the site for some time. Even after a year a few arms retained a degree of green plumpness, but eventually these too began to ooze and deflate

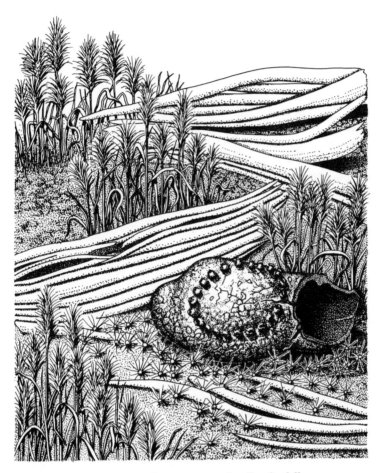

Drying spring grasses turn brown among the ribs of a fallen saguaro.

under the desert sun. The pleated skin of the cactus turned brown and began to crack and flake away from the trunk and arms of the giant, exposing the durable ribs and tough saguaro "boots," the cylinders of firm scar tissue that form when Gila woodpeckers excavate nests in living saguaros.

Now, in the first days of summer, the grasses that once created a green outline of the giant saguaro corpse have begun to die their own natural deaths. For the moment, they hold their tufted heads erect in the spaces among the flattened ribs of a fallen arm. A windrow of metallic grey spines rests in the lee of the still-substantial trunk, a skeletal trunk totally bereft of the fleshy water-storing coat that helped make the saguaro giant immune to decades of summer droughts before sustaining one brief generation of flies.

Black Plumage – Desert Heat

My arms are beaded with sweat as I labor up a hillside in the Usery Mountains. Even at this early morning hour the sun seems intent on burning a hole through the shirt on my back.

A tarantula hawk wasp with the dreamy name of *Pepsis thisbe* sails past on its way to an early-blooming acacia, where it circles once and twice before flying off in the buoyant manner of its species, its long hindlegs trailing behind. On its way downhill it weaves between two living saguaros that stand monumentally above the acacias and jojobas.

Up ahead, a chunky flycatcher dives off its ocotillo perch and races on powerful wings toward an unknowing victim. With an authoritative snap of its beak at the end of its dive, the flycatcher loops back like a yo-yo on a string to the perch it so recently left. Holding a large fly in its beak, the bird sharply thwacks the captured prey against the spiny stalk at its feet. The now-senseless fly is positioned headfirst in the bird's beak and neatly swallowed.

This is an olive-sided flycatcher, a bird usually associated with cold boreal forests of muskeg and old man's beard lichen, a brown bird that gives its territorial call from the tops of conifers. The bird books describe the male's cheeky whistle as "hip hip three cheers," or "hip hip three beers," depending on the mood or drinking habits of the translator.

Here in the desert the olive-sided flycatcher is a silent transient, on migration to a nest site in the Rockies or Canada. Despite the competence of the bird in snapping up desert insects, the flycatcher seems misplaced among the palo verdes, barrel cacti, and ocotillo stalks, where the temperature is in the nineties, instead of ornamenting a dead pine stub by a cool northern swamp.

Another eye-catching, dark-plumaged bird of the late spring is the phainopepla. There is no question that this is a genuine desert species because it breeds here as late as May. Down in the washes where the mistletoes grow, the "wheep wheep" (or "whurp whurp") of phainopeplas is a characteristic Sonoran Desert sound, and the sight of a glossy black male perched at the top of a mesquite or palo verde is a characteristic Sonoran Desert image. But why should a desert bird be jet black? Admittedly, phainopeplas do not stick it out through the really rough part of the summer, departing instead for northern Arizona, California, New Mexico or Texas for a second bout of breeding in June, returning to central Arizona only in September or later. Nevertheless, May and September are not cool months in the desert; even then, male phainopeplas insist on sitting out in the full sun on elevated perches as if the heat were of no concern to them.

When I hike the desert on hot days I select pale clothing, an old faded shirt, a pair of tan khakis tufted by run-ins with thorny catclaw acacias, a hat of any color except black. My fondness for khakis, which extends beyond desert hikes, has earned me the derision of my fashion-conscious teenaged sons and amused comments from my colleagues. I suffer these criticisms calmly, because I know from long experience that I will be comfortable and relatively cool in a pair of baggy, beat-up, unstylish khakis.

If, however, khakis were black, I could not imagine wearing them on desert hikes in May or even April. But there sits a jet black male phainopepla on an absolutely exposed perch, showing no sign of distress under the roasting sun.

My colleague, Glenn Walsberg, knows why the India ink plumage of male phainopeplas is no handicap to them in their environment, and his discoveries show that a prejudice against black desert apparel may have to be carefully qualified. In one of Walsberg's

The male phainopepla has blacker plumage than its mate.

projects on the thermal consequences of having coats of different colors, he compared heat gain in male and female phainopeplas. Females would seem to be more sensibly attired for desert living because they are a pale grey rather than the flashy black of their mates. As most of us would expect, the female's dull plumage does indeed reflect substantially more sunlight — two to three times more — than the male's black coat. As most of us would *not* expect, however, temperatures at the skin surface of male and female phainopeplas are only marginally different under most conditions.

You may wonder how Walsberg persuaded phainopeplas to reveal the temperatures of their bodies beneath their feathers. To do so, he had to first shoot a number of the birds, after securing the necessary permits. He then carefully skinned his specimens. The featherless and skinless body of the phainopepla was made to adopt the position of a perching bird, and a copper cast of the body was constructed. Once the hollow cast had been made, the skin and feathers were reattached to the copper "body" with a firm adhesive, and thermocouples were placed inside the copper cast. These devices permitted Walsberg to measure the temperature under the skin of the mounted specimen.

Walsberg took the copper, skin and feather models of phainopeplas to the field, where he placed them on the tops of palo verdes in full sunshine on hot days in April. The thermocouple readings revealed that underneath their plumage, males were only one to two degrees centigrade warmer than females.

This counterintuitive result occurs because all the solar radiation absorbed in the feathers is not passed on to the skin and body. Some of it is carried off by various processes before it ever gets to phainopepla flesh. For example, even light winds carry away a considerable amount of the heat absorbed in the outer surfaces of black feathers before the heat can travel down the shaft to the skin. Therefore, the outermost surface of a black male phainopepla may be much hotter than the surface of a pale grey female, but a male is only a little warmer where it counts, at skin level. The effective temperature difference between males and females caused by their color differences is so small that it is probably biologically trivial. When it is really scorching, males simply head for the shade within a mesquite or orient their bodies to present a smaller surface area to the sun. In this way they keep as cool on the inside as their mates.

But what if phainopeplas were white instead of grey or black? Surely then phainopeplas would be much cooler. Not necessarily, as Walsberg and his coworkers have shown by taking advantage of natural variation in pigeons to study the thermal effects of black versus white plumage. Solar radiation contains a considerable short-wave component, and these wavelengths penetrate more easily through white feathers than through black feathers, which trap short-wave radiation in their outer layers. The heat transferred directly to the skin of a white-feathered pigeon is trapped beneath the coat of feathers. The bottom line is that if it is even slightly windy, a black pigeon's heat load *at its skin surface* will be less than that of a white-plumaged bird. By keeping solar radiation from penetrating deeply, black feathers hold the heat on the surface, where air moving past the bird can carry it away.

Actually, white birds and white mammals are uncommon in the desert, which supports the argument that thermal demands of desert living may actually favor dark rather than white coats. Furthermore, desert-dwelling Bedouin tribesmen, a people very much at home in a superheated climate, commonly wear black robes. Although dark robes in sunshine reach much higher temperatures than do white ones, the skin temperatures of black-garbed Bedouins are no greater than those wearing white robes. Bedouins wear two sets of robes, and it is thought that air movement between the outer and inner robe is responsible for the absence of a thermal penalty for wearing black.

Even if Bedouin outerwear were available at the local Army/Navy surplus, I would not trade in my tattered khakis for a pair of black robes, a decision that I know my sons will greet with relief. But at least male phainopeplas are not violating common sense as they sit cockily on the top of a palo verde while I plod past under an unforgiving sun, daydreaming about the latest in refrigerated khaki outfits.

Goatsucker Myths?

In the early morning the temperature is almost pleasant, especially in the deeply cut washes with their pockets of cooler air. On the flat plain, saguaros cast elongate images of themselves over the palo verdes and chollas, shadows that lie on the red and grey gravel of the desert floor.

A tarantula hawk wasp flies down a wash, dipping in and out of the shadows, cruising around each acacia before sailing on to the next spiny shrub. Many acacias now sport furry, pale yellow flowers, and their overly sweet, almost decadent perfume clots in the still air. Squat black flies and delicate grey butterflies sit side by side, probing the flowers urgently.

On the terminal arm of a ridge running down from the Usery Mountains a lesser nighthawk flushes from its perch on a fallen limb of a palo verde. It circles at a safe distance, using the palo verdes as a diaphanous shield, gliding, gliding, then snapping its wings sharply to provide energy for the next several yards of flight. It appears almost to float in the air, its wings held in a pronounced V, accenting its wing snaps with strange, gargled churrs of alarm.

A couple of years ago a lesser nighthawk nested in this same spot, and perhaps the circling nighthawk has a nest here today; if so, it is well hidden. The nighthawk turns on stiff wings to drift behind a jumbled pile of rocks, where it settles out of sight.

It is not easy to find the nests of lesser nighthawks. Like most other members of the goatsucker family, the Caprimulgidae, the female lesser nighthawk lays two eggs directly on the ground in a spot that she modifies hardly at all. The eggs are mottled in a classic grey and brown camouflage that helps the blotched eggs merge into their stony background when they are left unguarded. When the parent bird incubates the eggs, the parent's own vermiculite plumage of brown and white conceals the adult and its offspring to perfection. The nighthawk sits with its big eyes nearly shut, concealing the one conspicuous feature that might give it away to a passing coyote or desert fox.

An incubating bird is reluctant to leave its nest, permitting a predator or human to come very close before finally jumping up to power away on long white-banded wings. When I stumble upon a nighthawk nest I usually am just about to step on the incubating adult, which flutters away at the absolute last moment, exposing its hidden eggs.

Once I picked a nest for repeated inspections. Marking the spot mentally, I managed to find it again at three- and four-day intervals, each time flushing the bird when I was within a few yards of the nest. I very much wanted to see the youngsters, which are said to possess magnificent downy camouflage, but I was disappointed; on my fourth trip to the nest I found nothing at all.

I judged that had the eggs hatched, the "nestlings" (if one could call the scrape on the ground a nest) would surely be present, for they would be too young to move. Their absence led me to conclude that a wandering predator had found the nest and feasted on lesser nighthawk eggs, or hatchlings, or perhaps even a lesser nighthawk adult, although there were no scattered brown and white feathers on the ground. I felt a twinge of guilt, because bird nests visited regularly by humans are more likely to fail than those that are checked only at long intervals. Perhaps my frequent trips to the nest had tipped off a watching thrasher or some other egg consumer, which had taken advantage of the lesser nighthawk after I had left.

That Christmas my parents gave me *The Birds of Arizona* as a present. The book contains a comprehensive list of the species found in Arizona, with a brief sketch of each species' distribution in the state and information on its natural history. It is the kind of present that only a longtime birder can appreciate, and even I did not sit down at once to read the tome from cover to cover. I did, however, browse here and there, admiring the center section of color plates by Elliot Porter, picking up a tidbit of information on Abert's towhee, a scrap on the grey hawk.

In the course of my literary grazing I came to the species account for the lesser nighthawk. There I read that the bird sometimes moves its eggs from a disturbed nest site to a new location. I felt better at once, thinking that perhaps I failed to find the eggs because the parent, irritated by my visits, had shifted them to a safe new spot unknown to me.

But how? Nighthawks can hardly be expected to move their eggs with their feet, which are tiny and weak, nor is it easy to imagine how they might successfully use their heads or chests to nudge the eggs any distance across desert terrain. One mistake and the nighthawk would send its egg careening out of control down a slope to disaster.

Perhaps, however, nighthawks move eggs by carrying them in their mouths. The mouths of lesser nighthawks and their goatsucker relatives are large enough to perform this task. Although the beak of the bird appears small and unexceptional, when one inspects a nighthawk at close range (ideally in the hand) one finds that the gape of the bird is immense, a huge maw surrounded by stiff bristles, the better to sweep up the large flying insects that the bird pursues at dawn and dusk.

The common name "goatsucker" is an Americanism (the British prefer the more refined "nightjar") based on the American myth that the great mouths of caprimulgids enable the birds to engulf a goat's teat and steal its milk at night. In fact, the birds are strict insectarians and have no interest in milk of any sort, let alone that produced by goats.

The possibility that goatsuckers might use their mouths to shift eggs from one site to another piqued my curiosity, and I decided to see whether the behavior had ever been carefully documented. According to *Birds of the World,* there have been persistent reports ever since Audubon's days of egg-carrying in various caprimulgids. But what about lesser nighthawks *per se?* The authors of *The Birds of Arizona* did not cite a specific reference in the scientific literature on egg-moving by lesser nighthawks. Instead, the claim was followed only by the name Levy in parentheses.

A trip to the *Zoological Record,* a massive set of reference volumes that, among other things, lists all the scientific papers written about birds in a given year, revealed that one Seymour H. Levy had published a number of notes in journals like the *Auk* and the *Condor,* solid ornithological outlets, on new species seen in Arizona. I guessed that this had to be the same Levy mentioned in the lesser nighthawk account, but I failed to turn up a paper under his name on the behavior of this bird.

A letter from Gale Monson, one of the authors of *The Birds of Arizona,* yielded the news that Seymour H. Levy was indeed the person who had reported on egg-moving nighthawks and that he was a meticulous observer. I called Mr. Levy, who still lives in Tucson, and learned that he had on at least one and probably several occasions located lesser nighthawk nests, only to have the eggs moved a short time after he had flushed the incubating adult. He recalled that when he went back to the nest on the day of his discovery, the eggs had been shifted, not far — only a yard or two — but far enough to force him to hunt around a bit. Unfortunately, he was not present to see how the adult managed to move the eggs.

Mildly encouraged by this turn of events, I decided to continue my search for information. The section on Caprimulgidae in the 1985 volume of the *Zoological Record* listed a paper by H. O. Jackson, published in the *Wilson Bulletin,* the journal of the Wilson Ornithological Society. I knew I had hit paydirt when I read the title: "Commentary and observations on the alleged transportation of eggs and young by caprimulgids." I wasted no time in tracking this paper down. I read that despite claims that Audubon had seen a chuck-wills-widow, a goatsucker of the southeastern United States, move its clutch in its mouth, there was no evidence that Audubon had observed egg-transport personally. Instead, he probably had heard it at second hand from an informant who may have been inspired to stretch things a bit, to put it as charitably as Jackson did.

Jackson was unable to locate a single verified case of egg-moving by a caprimulgid of any sort. He concluded: "The 'capacious mouth' of a nightjar could certainly accommodate an egg, perhaps even two, just as it could probably accommodate the teat of a goat, but there appears to be no more evidence of it being an egg-carrier than there is of it being a goatsucker."

Jackson's own research focused on the fiery-necked nightjar of Zimbabwe, which he studied specifically to determine whether these birds moved their eggs. He used pink nail varnish to mark the clutches at several dozen nests and flagged the location of each nest, but he never found a marked egg in a new location. If the same is true of the lesser nighthawk, then I should feel guilty anew. Tucked in Jackson's paper, however, was an escape hatch for me. I had imagined young nighthawks to be relatively helpless creatures, sure to remain in their nest for some days after hatching. This is not the case; downy baby caprimulgids, out of the egg only a few hours, are mobile and can crawl to a new spot if their parents call for them. Therefore, my failure to locate the nestlings did not necessarily mean that they had been devoured between my visits (although this is still a strong possibility). I like to imagine them crouched safely under an incubating adult tucked out of sight in the lee of a little bursage on the day I came searching unsuccessfully for them.

A nonbeliever in egg-transport by nightjars, Jackson sought to explain how such accounts might arise, pointing to three possibilities. First, movements of an incubating adult might cause the eggs to roll a short distance, leading to small shifts in the location of a clutch over time. Second, an observer might encounter a replacement clutch of a pair whose first nest had been discovered by an egg-eating predator. The observer might conclude, incorrectly, that the replacement clutch was the first set of eggs moved to a new nest site. Third, an observer might simply make an error in remembering where a nest was, reaching the faulty conclusion that the site had been shifted, when it had not been changed at all.

Jackson's arguments are persuasive, although Seymour Levy's account of finding lesser nighthawk eggs shifted within hours of discovery of the nest would seem to rule out the possibility of type two and type three errors. Furthermore, the lesser nighthawk is a different species than the fiery-necked nightjar; perhaps a systematic study might confirm that the nighthawk does move its eggs at least a short distance from the spot on which they had been laid. I note that the recently published *A Field Guide to the Nests, Eggs, and Nestlings of North American Birds* repeats the claim that nightjars in general can move their eggs and young in the vicinity of the nest, although this source does not specify the mode of transport or provide supporting references for the claim.

We seem to have arrived at the point in the exploration of egg-transport by caprimulgids at which biologists are likely to announce sagely that more research is needed to resolve the issue. Let me second that. And may whoever decides to hunt for the nests of lesser nighthawks be possessed of much patience, keen eyesight, and the willingness to demolish an intriguing myth, either by showing that nighthawks definitely do not move their eggs or by showing that the story is true, after all, and so can be classified as a myth no longer.

Empress Butterflies: Hooked on Hackberry

At the Salt River very early this morning, before the sun has had its chance to cook the desert, the water sweeps along at a comfortable clip, rippling the surface of the shallows, eddying back to undercut the sandy bank of the floodplain. The narrow mesquite bosque bordering both sides of the river looks green and wild from a vantage high on Coon's Bluff.

Over the surface of the water a great company of birds circles and glides. At first they seem to be swallows, but they are lesser nighthawks behaving like giant swallows, their white wing patches flashing as they twist and turn. Up and down the river, hundreds of nighthawks feast on the hatch of an aquatic insect, perhaps a mayfly or a midge or some other tiny insect sufficient in number to have attracted a huge assembly of lesser nighthawks. The dancing birds are silent as they singlemindedly pursue their prey. A great blue heron belches out a rude squawk as it labors upstream.

The Salt River is linked to the desert by a great network of washes, bone-dry now and almost always. Only after an exceptional thunderstorm will muddy water spill along a wash and add itself to the regulated flow of the river.

The gravel of a wash that feeds the river is pocked with the foot-prints of peccaries and jackrabbits, the tracks of Gambel's quail and curve-billed thrashers, spoor accumulated since the last big rain. When it rained, a sufficient number of rivulets slid down hillsides to coalesce in a thin, foamy runoff that ventured partway down the wash toward the river. The place where the temporary stream pe-tered out is marked by a static wave of displaced gravel and sand, frozen in place as a signal that the wash had finally seen some ac-tion. It has been a long time since the gravel in this wash was re-arranged and smoothed, and so prepared to make a fresh record of activity in a highway of the desert.

Many animals travel back and forth along the wash, perhaps be-cause it is the path of least resistance, offering smooth, packed sand rather than uneven rocky slopes with loose stones and sharp gullies. Because the traveling is good, and also because the vegetation is thicker on the borders of the washes, a hike along a wash usually yields a rich supply of surprises.

A great-horned owl flops off a perch on a rocky ledge overlook-ing the dry desert highway and flies silently downstream, turning sharply to angle behind a green mesquite. A pair of verdins chips in alarm.

A squat lizard sprints noisily from the edge of the wash, across the mound of sticks a woodrat calls home, and scrambles up an ironwood trunk. *Sceloporous magister* is the largest, wariest lizard in this part of the desert, where the still bigger desert iguana is absent. It disappears among a maze of limbs in the ironwood.

Helicoptering along the waterless wash, a dragonfly looks out of place. It is here to feed on the smaller insects that occupy the spiny vegetation, including hackberry bushes, some of which grow on marginal islands in the middle of the streambed. These big shrubs or small trees, wide and thick as they are tall, look like giant tumble-weeds covered with a disordered blanket of dark green leaves.

At almost every large hackberry a small orange-brown butterfly perches on the ground, ready to jump from the open gravel near the tree and skitter away in a flurry of wingbeats, only to circle back and land near its original perching site. As one butterfly sits with its wings spread on the pale floor of the wash, another hackberry butterfly zips around the bush. Instantly the perched butterfly snaps into flight and darts toward its fellow, which leads it on a brief but sprightly chase away from the hackberry. Shortly a butter-

A male empress butterfly, prepared to defend its territory against other males, perches on the ground near a hackberry bush.

fly comes gliding back toward the tree to land again nearby. What is going on? Is the returnee the same individual that perched there before? Male or female? And why is the empress butterfly so fond of hackberry trees?

My colleague Ron Rutowski knows the answers to these questions because he and his assistants have spent considerable time trying to untangle the social system of empress butterflies. A key element in their program of research has been to mark captured individuals with a felt-tipped pen.

Male and female empress butterflies look superficially the same from a distance, although females are somewhat larger than males on average and their flight is less hyperactive. But in the hand, after removal from an insect net, males can be positively identified; on the undersides of the tips of their abdomens they possess distinctive claspers used to hold the tip of the female's abdomen during copulation.

Rutowski found that the butterflies alertly poised on the ground near a hackberry bush are always males. After being marked, males sometimes return to their bushes, where they remain for only thirty minutes or so on an April or May morning. Some, but not many, will return on a number of other days to the same spot. During their brief stays the males are definitely territorial, pursuing all intruder males of their species and usually chasing them away.

But why should males go to the trouble to defend a hackberry shrub and the surrounding gravel? Perhaps because female empress butterflies lay their eggs strictly on the foliage of this plant. It follows that males are guaranteed to encounter females if they wait by attractive hackberry bushes, which will be frequented by gravid females searching for sites on which to lay their eggs. But will these females be receptive to the sexual advances of males?

In order to answer this question, Rutowski captured, killed, and dissected a sample of females flying in the washes to see how many times they had copulated. One can read the sexual histories of dissected female butterflies because they receive and store a large, durable structure called a spermatophore from each male with whom they mate. The spermatophore is a packet that, depending on the butterfly species, weighs two to eight percent of the male's body weight, not a trivial amount. The spermatophore contains sperm and nutrients that females may use by degrees over a period of many days. Even after the spermatophore has been depleted of its sperm and other contents, the shrunken, wrinkled external covering of the package remains within the female. Inspection of a female's bursa copulatrix, a large and distinctive pouch attached to her reproductive tract, will therefore reveal how many spermatophores a female has received, and thus how many mates the female has had in her adulthood.

The Rutowski Report on the sex lives of empress butterfly females is that they mate only once. Not one of the many females he has examined had more than one spermatophore within her bursa.

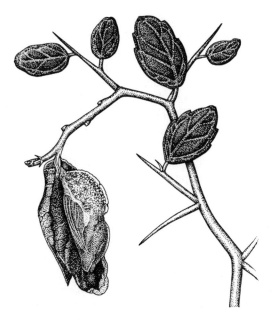

An empress butterfly pupa on a hackberry leaf.

This suggests that males are not hanging around hackberry bushes to encounter mature females that have already mated. If not, why are they there?

Hackberry bushes are the best places to meet newly emerged virgin females that have grown up feasting on hackberry leaves and have pupated in the shelter of the plant. The pupae even look like hackberry leaves, a camouflage that helps them hide from the many birds that would enjoy an exotic meal of empress butterfly pupae. Moreover, although most other butterfly pupae begin to change color one or two days before the adult emerges, empress butterfly pupae remain unchanged, green and hackberry-leaflike, until the last few hours before emergence. Pupae can "afford" to mimic only hackberry leaves because they develop from larvae guaranteed to have lived only on this plant.

Males that station themselves by hackberry bushes probably do better at meeting females than do males that search elsewhere, particularly if males can time their wait to match the period when virgin females are most likely to take their first flights. Under laboratory conditions, females emerge from the chrysalis before dawn. If the same is true for females in nature, they will undergo metamorphosis in darkness, when their movements cannot be seen by keen-sighted predators. After expanding and hardening their wings, virgin females probably are ready to begin their maiden voyages sometime in the early morning. This is precisely when males are most likely to be waiting for them; the competition among males for hackberry territories peaks between 8:00 and 10:00 A.M.

We would also expect males to fight most fiercely for the bushes with the highest concentration of female pupae, provided there was some way they could identify such hackberry bushes, perhaps on the basis of size or luxuriance of foliage. There is no doubt that males prefer some trees to others. In Rutowski's study two particularly popular hackberries had a male in residence on seventy-three percent of his censuses (made at half-hour intervals during the mornings of seventeen days). The other nineteen bushes on his route had a combined occupancy rate of only fourteen percent. Moreover, at the popular spots males often had to give up "their" trees to persistent intruders, whereas at other sites males generally stayed as long as they wanted and then voluntarily abandoned the spot.

Unfortunately, in empress butterflies as in many other species, the probability that a female will metamorphose into an adult in a given host plant on a given day is very small. Therefore, Rutowski did not see a sufficient number of matings to test his hypothesis that males are more likely to defend certain sites because mating chances are highest there. But he did show that females were more commonly seen at the male-preferred sites, suggesting that these popular trees were more attractive to ovipositing females and, therefore, should contain more larvae, more pupae, and — eventually — more emerging virgins.

Like the miniature fruit flies of the Sonoran Desert, the far-from-showy empress butterflies are easy to overlook and may seem insignificant, but their behavior tells us something about the global issue of how evolution operates. Empress butterflies, like cactophilic *Drosophila*, have highly specialized egg-laying requirements because their larvae feed on a severely restricted diet. As a result, adult females are found predictably where the larval food occurs, and males compete to monopolize these sites because they reliably yield mates. Dependence on hackberries creates a pattern of distribution of females, and males have evolved adaptive responses to this pattern. There is a method in their maleness, design in their actions, meaning in their fondness for certain perches scattered along a dry desert wash in May.

Flash Flood

In May it is almost impossible to imagine water flowing down the washes near Usery Mountain and around the hackberries growing there. The monsoon season seems light years away and the sand of the washes as ancient and dry as a Saharan dune. But in August enough rain may fall in a short enough period to send a few inches of water surging along channels that drain the Usery Mountain watershed. Driving out to the desert the day after such a rain, I will see sheets of damp sand deposited on the blacktop and ditches that have been gouged a little deeper by rushing water. But the streams run for only a short time, and the only sign of water will be a brown pool or two along the roadside. The pools quickly evaporate, leaving a residue of smooth mud in their place.

The brevity and modest flow of most flash floods in central Arizona is such that I rarely have seen a dry wash flowing and I never have seen a true wall of water coming down a dry wash at the start of a flood. But once in southern Utah, on a grey monsoon day in early August, I almost became a part of a flash flood.

Clouds had coalesced over the Bear's Ears Mesa miles to the east of White Canyon; white sheets of rain soon blocked neighboring hills from view. At the trailhead, however, skies were only overcast; there was an occasional sprinkle, but the day was calm. In the flat, sombre light the shadowless canyon seemed more monumental than ever, even intimidating in the grand scale of its construction. The trail left the juniper-dotted plateau and dropped down through white, cross-cut canyon walls to reach the dry creek more than five hundred feet below.

Once at the bottom of the narrow canyon, the trail skirted the empty streambed, cutting from one side to the other. Slickrock walls towered above the little strip of willows, oaks and cottonwoods growing along the watercourse. About fifteen minutes down the trail I heard an unfamiliar sound that I decided must be a wind sweeping high overhead off the plateau. The noise was not loud, but it was persistent, steady, odd. I walked on unconcerned. For a minute or two the whispering noise held steady, but as the flood flashed round a bend upstream the sound became horribly louder all at once.

When I realized that an indeterminate but clearly considerable amount of water was headed my way like an express train, I was on a little meander in the canyon on a stretch of sand and scrub bordered on one side by the wash and on the other by canyon walls. In the few moments before the flood reached me I ran in panic downstream along the wash looking for a way up the canyon on my right, but the sheer rock walls leaned out toward the wash, forming an unclimbable obstacle. I then had the choice of trying to cross the wash to reach the other side before the water thundered through or of heading for the highest point on my side of the stream. The thought of being caught midstream was so unappealing that I stayed on my side and scrambled frantically through a patch of scrub oak about thirty feet from the edge of the wash next to the imprisoning grey canyon wall. After climbing the biggest oak, which was disappointingly small, I was about six feet off the ground just as the wall of water came around the last bend upstream. Because of the screen of vegetation, I could not see the flood from my vantage, but as I contemplated the vagaries of existence I could hear with terrible clarity the crunch of boulders smashing along the streambed and the crack of limbs ripped from trees.

Seconds later the roar of the flood's leading wall traveled past and around the downstream bend, leaving me alive but shaken by the experience. I waited a bit before descending to inspect the flood. A light rain misted my glasses. Where streambed had been, there was now a torrential rush of water from ten to forty feet across and about four feet deep. The rampaging stream consisted of one part of Navajo red sandstone, finely ground, to one part of water, topped with foam, the whole thing whipped into a frenzy. It would have been suicidal to try to cross the stream at once, and I knew that the waters would recede eventually.

For the time being I was trapped, and if another storm hit the Bear's Ears there could be another flood. I most definitely did not want to be up the little oak tree if the main event was preparing for a grand entry somewhere up the canyon even then. Hustling about my little Devil's Island, I discovered one barely possible route to a spot high on the canyon wall that I might head for if I heard the big one coming down White Canyon. I did not look forward to becoming a rock climber under these conditions. As I waited on a little ledge above the floodplain I admired a nicely sheltered spot an easy climb one hundred feet up a sloping hillside across the impassable stream, and I reproached myself for not immediately seeking safety as soon as I had heard that strange whispering sound.

The floodwaters carried with them an unusual and unpleasant odor, slightly acrid, a bit like witch hazel, a smell of fear and anxiety. The red-brown waters thudded into the rock walls that checked their course and pulled at the willows in their way.

The drizzle stopped and the roaring stream receded with painful slowness. As the afternoon passed torturously and grim shadows filled the canyon, a rock squirrel came out from somewhere to forage on the sandy meander and tiny red-dotted toads sat in moist crevices in the canyon wall. Ten feet above the current flood, masses of flotsam from a much more impressive flood in the past gripped cottonwoods in a fierce embrace. Had a wall of water of similar dimensions come down the canyon while I was there I knew I would have been on my way to feed the fishes in Lake Powell dozens of miles downstream.

In the late afternoon I gingerly waded across the relatively subdued stream. Silt clung to my legs up to my thighs when I left the water.

By the next morning the torrent had disappeared, leaving behind stranded logs, a trickling stream, and great rippled flats of fine sandstone mud. Dancing sunlight reflected from the remnant watercourse to overhanging canyon walls. A desert primrose poked out of the mud with leaves mangled and muddied, its stem draped with flash-flood debris. The plant had bloomed overnight and its cheerful yellow flower faced upstream, looking toward the sun and the source of future floods.

Broom-rapes, Cancer-roots, and Strangle-vetches

A red-tail hawk circles on a shimmering updraft, rising farther and farther above a mousey rock wren that trills and pipes from a superheated boulder. The wren bobs and ducks out of view, and pops up in a new rocky outpost for another burst of song. The saguaros have begun to bloom, and some balance a bouquet of as many as a dozen creamy white flowers on a limb tip or trunk top. Most, however, have only round green flower buds, waiting for their opening night and day in the desert.

A cicada screeches in alarm as it explodes out of a little bursage, a nondescript grey-green plant with masses of small yellow-green burrs. The insect manages to sound surprisingly like a rattlesnake, enough so to send me jumping out of my hiking boots as I, too, take to the air, if only for a second. Bursage is the commonest shrublet on the hillside and, for that matter, in all the upland Sonoran Desert. Unlike the larger brittlebush or the fairy-duster or the saguaro, all of which have conspicuous, attractive flowers and a host of animal pollinators, the local bursage is wind-pollinated and its small pale flowers blend into its foliage. As a result, humans pay little attention to the plant.

The broom-rape *Orobanche ludoviciana*, however, is fond of bursage, and for good reason; broom-rape is a parasitic plant that could not survive without a physical attachment to bursage. The generic name *Orobanche* is taken from two Greek words that mean "strangle" and "vetch." The genus is a large one with many European species, some of which are important pests of peas and clover, as well as of tomatoes and melons. All the members of the genus make a living at some other plant's expense.

There, growing under a bursage, is a specimen of the parasite, pale brown and fleshy, without a trace of green chlorophyll. The visible part of the plant is its flowering stalk, a few inches high, a stem whose leaves have been reduced to scales, the flowers small, touched with purple. The plant is reminiscent of Indian pipe, a parasite of eastern woodlands unrelated to *O. ludoviciana* that has independently evolved a similar form.

The rest of the parasite is underground, including its most important component, the haustorium, a rather ponderous name given

Broom-rape is a parasitic plant that relies on bursage for nutrients.

to the structure that attaches to roots of the bursage and permits
the broom-rape to live off the fruits of its host's labors. The haustorium develops quickly when a broom-rape seed germinates. The
parasite's seeds are tiny and are produced in vast quantities when
the flowers of the parasite are pollinated. Although minute, *Orobanche* seeds are wonderfully sculptured with many ridges and cavities. Job Kuijt, a specialist in parasitic plants, believes the function
of this elaborate carving is to create air spaces that buoy the seeds
on rivulets of water during a rainstorm. As the seeds ride trickles
of rainwater, they are dispersed and drawn into cracks in the soil.

Most of the seeds fortuitiously carried down into the ground during a thunderstorm in the desert will never germinate. Only those that, by a multiplication of good fortune, not only are buried but also happen to come to rest near the root of a bursage have a chance to produce a mature parasite.

A seed that comes near a host begins to germinate, perhaps because of a stimulating chemical diffusing from the roots of the host. The germinated parasitic seed produces a proliferation of cells that move toward the root, contact it, and delicately penetrate it, forming a perfect graft with the host plant. The almost imperceptible connection taps the root, forming a conduit that siphons off the products of bursage photosynthesis, which instead of fueling its own root growth and development help the parasite grow. *Orobanche* also steal minerals and water from the roots they invade.

There is no question that broom-rapes harm agricultural plants, and no reason to doubt that they act as a damaging drain on the bursages unlucky enough to harbor them. One organism's parasite, however, is another's boon. Some beetle larvae consume the short, fleshy roots of certain *Orobanche*, and Kuijt suspects that ants, for example, would enjoy cutting up and eating the flowering parts of *Orobanche* if they could reach them. The parasite may be able to thwart most ants, however, by covering the approaches to its flowers with a mass of little sticky obstacles. Unfortunately, no one has done rigorous experiments to show whether these glandular projections do, in fact, deter foraging ants, of which there are many in the desert.

The defenses of *Orobanche* clearly do not work against all possible consumers; the Indians of the arid southwestern United States once ate them or used them to produce medicinal potions. They dabbed the parasite's stem on sores, thus the name cancer-root. For better or for worse, *Orobanche* no longer need contend with humans, but they still are targeted by some herbivores, perhaps by small rodents or even peccaries. Whoever the mystery animals may be, they seem able to detect the plant even before it has broached the surface of the soil. I rarely find an *Orobanche* rising from the surface of the ground, but more commonly discover places where some creature has excavated a pit four to six inches deep, uncovering one or more stalks, which it consumes entirely or in part. When another stem emerges from a pit of this sort, it rarely lasts more than a day or two before it, too, has disappeared, chopped off at the base. This miniature asparagus of the desert should be a great delicacy for a woodrat, for it is fleshy and moist at a time of year when little else is.

We do not become indignant when a woodrat, if that is what it is, eats a broom-rape, but there is something about a parasite that makes us feel judgmental. The thought of an *Orobanche* stealthily grafting itself to bursage seems positively insidious. Perhaps this is because we consume things forthrightly, out in the open, like woodrats, and must contend, like woodrats, with secretive internal parasites that tap our largess almost without our knowing what is happening. To call a fellow human a parasite is an insult, whereas no one hurls "Omnivore!" at a rival in the heat of an argument. But if *Orobanche* could classify the organisms in its environment, they probably would vilify woodrats or whatever it is that digs them up, while flattering themselves that their manner of making a living is more admirable, even more moral, than that of creatures who must clumsily destroy the foods on which they depend.

Freedom Fighters

In this early morning in mid-May a large grey bee traveling at high speed crashes headlong into my cheek. I recoil from the impact. The bee dashes away, none the worse for wear as it continues its journey through a mesquite forest growing by the Salt River in central Arizona. The open woodland of expansive mesquites and big blue palo verdes occupies the Salt River floodplain, creating a narrow ribbon of greenery surrounded by the austere and waterless landscape of the upland Sonoran Desert. The rocky barren hillsides rimming the mesquite bosque are dotted with stunted foothills palo verdes and spiny teddy-bear cholla cacti.

All around sail hundreds more of the beautiful pearly grey digger bees, *Centris pallida*, as big as bumblebees and just as noisy; they make the riparian woodland resonate with their humming. Although a few bees zoom past at head level, the vast majority cruise in sinuous loops within a few centimeters of the surface of the earth, flying just over the short brown grasses and the sandy tracks cut by offroad vehicles. In the open areas between mesquites there are so many digger bees that they create a thin blanket of life that appears to float above the ground. It is a blanket always on the move, its pattern always changing.

Here and there the blanket unravels a little as a bee drops out of the flying mass and descends to the ground. Most dropouts walk quickly in little circles before buzzing up to rejoin the fabric of their fellows. But some begin to dig urgently, using their front legs to propel soil out behind them. As the excavation deepens, the digging bee begins to gnaw at the hard-packed earth before hurling the loosened material under its body and out of the pit.

When I first saw a digger bee at work (in a May more than a decade ago), I assumed that I was watching a female in the early stages of building her nest. I was dead wrong, although *Centris pallida* is a ground-nesting species whose females make lovely, amphora-shaped brood pots at the ends of short tunnels that descend into the soil. Females gather nectar and pollen from palo verde and ironwood flowers to place in their brood pots. Once an underground pot is about two-thirds full, the female lays an egg on the surface of the thick syrup, seals the clay brood pot, fills the slanted nest tunnel with loose soil, and goes on to build another burrow nest elsewhere. The egg left behind hatches in the brood pot, and the larva consumes the food its mother provided. If all goes well, the larva passes through a series of stages underground, ultimately reaching adulthood nearly a year after its mother deposited it as an egg.

The digger bees I watch today, like those I saw years ago, are not nesting. They are *all* males, thousands of them scattered in pockets over an area much bigger than a football field. One of the males on the ground begins to throw soil behind him with an almost frantic air and another bee joins him. The digger stops and turns to face the newcomer, they rear up with legs spread, and then topple together to wrestle on the ground. While they fight, buzzing with a high-pitched ferocity, a third male arrives to poke his head into the digging pit. Just as the new arrival begins to dig, one of the two combatants returns to bump him emphatically away from the hole. And so the excavation continues, with frequent interruptions, until after about five minutes of work a neat shaft less than an inch long leads straight down into the earth. The current owner of the site has been digging steadily for a half-minute, having chased off his fellow males, when he suddenly pauses and backs up to stand on stilted legs over the burrow. From within comes a staccato "bzz-bzz" and shortly another bee, a female, bursts out of the hole, sending the sand flying. The digger male quickly mounts the emerging bee and copulates with her on the ground.

I have witnessed this feat many, many times, but I still feel like applauding a fighting male's skill in somehow locating and freeing a female from a tunnel under nearly an inch of Sonoran Desert soil.

After pausing for just a few seconds to couple, the male whirs his wings and the pair takes flight, the male holding the female with his legs and gripping her with his jaws just behind her head. As they gain altitude, they are pursued by another male, which strikes them in midair. The pair tumbles out of control to the earth. There they are instantly set upon by their aerial assailant, and soon by a number of others, until a bundle of bees tumbles over the baked ground. As they struggle with each other their wings produce a collective whine that can be heard far away.

The eight or so bees in the bundle attempt to force their way to the female, and soon one bee breaks free from the group with his prize in his grip. He is an unusually large male and evidently has succeeded in usurping the female from her original partner, who is a large male but not as big as the bruiser who dwarfs the female he carries away. The male that lost his mate and the others quickly disband once the female has disappeared.

The new pair soars up into a nearby mesquite, where the male couples with the female. After withdrawing his genitalia, this male does not release his partner, but instead begins to generate a pleasant deep rattling sound, a post-copulatory "song" that he "sings" while rubbing the sides of the female with his legs in energetic strokes. He also thumps her lightly with his abdomen to the tune of his acoustical signal. After a couple of minutes of singing, the male opens his jaws and releases his hold on the female. He drops off and soon is back with the masses of males searching for another buried female.

The remarkable behavior of the digger bees prompted me and my coworkers, Gene Jones and Steve Buchmann, to ask how males locate females they cannot see. We quickly dismissed the hypothesis that females communicate with males by way of a special odor or *pheromone* that they release while in the incomplete emergence tun-

A male digger bee attempts to dig out an emerging virgin female, with whom it will mate.

nel. Evidence against this hypothesis came from the discovery that males excavate emerging males, as well as females. Males of the digger bee tend to come out somewhat earlier in the spring than females, but there is considerable overlap. As a result, some males are emerging when there are many mate-seeking males already aboveground. After a digger bee has dug down to an emerging male, he usually pauses and then draws back as the other male exits. During the peak of the emergence period, however, when the sexual frenzy among males is high, emerging males sometimes are mounted and even carried off to an elevated perch by the diggers that uncovered them, only to be released when it becomes clear that these bees cannot be mated. One has to resist the temptation to imagine that the digger male must be disappointed at having worked so hard just to dig up a fellow male.

To examine the cues used by males to locate underground objects, we did some simple experiments in which we buried dead specimens of *Centris pallida* in the emergence area. Males quickly found and excavated these items, and they did the same for buried dead honey bees. The indiscriminate digging of digger bee males also leads them to excavate females of other species of bees and wasps, and even a beetle that metamorphoses underground. These results indicate that males do not need a distinctive acoustical signal or even an odor characteristic of their species to find an underground individual. Instead, males appear to be hunting for chemical substances associated with insect bodies generally, odor cues that they can somehow detect at the surface of the ground, cues coming from buried objects that often, but not always, turn out to be receptive females of their species.

Having discovered how males find buried females, we wondered why males had evolved this extraordinary ability. To develop our hypothesis we used the Darwinian perspective on the evolution of animal behavior. Darwin realized that evolutionary change occurs when individuals differ in their ability to produce descendants, with each new generation shaped in the image of the most reproductively successful members of the preceding generation. If the behavior of male digger bees has been shaped by past selection, their actions should help them reproduce maximally. But why should the capacity to locate preemergent females have this consequence for males endowed with this special skill?

A key element in the evolution of digging for females may be that females of *Centris pallida* mate just once and then become unreceptive for the rest of their lives. If a male is to leave many surviving offspring, he must find and copulate with virgins whose eggs he can fertilize. This requirement inevitably generates competition among males for virgins, and in emergence areas there are many, many competitors present. The race to locate and monopolize virgins before other males can horn in has evidently favored males with such sensitive virgin-detectors that they can track down females before they have left their emergence tunnels and become available to the horde of males searching aboveground.

Digger bees practice an extreme version of the mate-finding tactics of empress butterfly males. The object of both insects is to find and monopolize virgins in order to fertilize their eggs, but digger males must contend with dozens or even hundreds of competitors, not with the handful of intruders that challenges a male empress butterfly for his place in the sun by a hackberry bush.

We can test our hypothesis — that digger bee skills are the product of pressures created by single-mating females and intense competition among males — by predicting that the same exceptional ability will have evolved in other species whose females mate just once (or at great intervals) and whose males aggregate densely in mating locations. In fact, male digger bees are not unique in their adeptness at sniffing out virgins. There are other bees, butterflies, wasps, mosquitoes, and thrips, to name a few, whose virgin females become unreceptive after mating and whose males compete with many opponents by finding females before they have emerged.

The struggle to gain access to virgins (and their eggs) appears to rule almost everything that males of these species do. For example, male digger bees do not concede mating rights to the first individual to reach a female. Instead, fights for possession of digging sites and for females themselves are the order of the day. Locating a buried female is just the initial step to fertilizing her eggs. The male must succeed in keeping other males from usurping the spot until the female can emerge, and then, even after mounting her, a male may be pulled and pushed from "his" female before he has a chance to inseminate her.

Even *after* copulation with a female, competition for her may continue for a short time, and this is when the male's song-and-dance routine has a role to play. When we first heard and saw this display, Steve Buchmann and I believed that we were watching a typical precopulatory courtship display; the usual pattern within the animal kingdom is for a male to provide some special, precopulatory signal to a female that may make her receptive to mating. But the digger bee does not behave in a typical fashion. Instead, when we observed pairings closely we realized that the male usually coupled with the female immediately after mounting her, and only then did he begin to stroke and "sing" to his partner. (Incidentally, we have never been able to find the apparatus that allows males to produce their soft rattling buzz).

Dissections of females separated from their partners immediately after the initial coupling show that they have received a full complement of sperm from their mate. Thus, the elaborate acoustical and tactile display occurs after females have been inseminated.

In searching for a possible function for the postcopulatory behavior of the digger bee, Buchmann and I wondered if it might not be a message from the male to the female designed to make her unreceptive to other males. To test this possibility, we captured a sample of pairs immediately after they had coupled. In some cases we carefully pulled the male from the back of the female before the male's display. Other pairs were permitted to complete copulation *and* some of the postcopulatory display phase before we separated them. Both kinds of females were held in individual vials briefly before being introduced to a new male in an insect net. The sexual drive of male digger bees being what it is, they were quick to pounce upon these females, but only those females that had *not* experienced a postcopulatory display permitted the males to copulate with them.

Females therefore require a male to signal to them *after* sperm transfer in order to lose their sexual receptivity. If a male is pulled from the female before he can sing to her, she will accept sperm from another male, diluting or superseding the gametes she has already received and reducing the first male's chances of producing descendants by her. The reproductive benefits for a male that maintains his position on a female even after inseminating her probably causes males to carry their females away from the emergence hole on the ground after the initial copulation. Although the flying pair is exposed to aerial assault, a male mounted on a female on the ground is even more vulnerable, given the army of males searching close to the earth. Bundles of males usually form when a single male discovers a pair on the ground and prevents the pair from taking off, permitting still others to join the tussle.

In the takeover fights, as well as in combat for possession of a digging site, large males enjoy a big advantage. The size differences among male digger bees are not subtle. Some individuals weigh three times as much as others, and the bigger bees have the strength to force their way through the melee around a pair to usurp the female and carry her off to a safe perch. As a result, when I measure the head-widths of males (head-width being a convenient body part to measure and one that is highly correlated with weight in digger bees) I find that copulating males usually are larger than males in the general population. (I collect random samples of males by sweeping my insect net through the population of males patrolling the emergence site).

In fact, the biggest males are larger than the largest females, a most unusual phenomenon in insects. When there is a sexual difference in body size in insects, the general rule is that the larger individuals will be females. The exceptions occur almost universally in species in which there is intense combat among males over females, a point that Darwin himself made long ago.

That large males are reproducing more than smaller ones raises an intriguing evolutionary problem: Why is there such dramatic size variation in the species? Although one might think that small males should be on their way out because of the reproductive advantages of large body size in such a combative species, small males are in no immediate danger of elimination. I measured samples of digger bees by the Salt River in 1976, 1982, and again in 1988. There has been no trend toward a larger body size; even though in all three years the average head-width of mating males has been much greater than that of the population as a whole, the average head-width of bees sampled randomly has remained about the same.

We must reexamine the assumptions underlying the expectation that the trait of large male body size should be increasing in frequency over time in digger bee populations. A key assumption of evolutionary scenarios is that the characteristic of interest can be inherited. Body size in bees, however, is determined largely environmentally, by the amount of food the larval bee consumes. Mother bees control the size of their progeny by regulating the quantity of provisions they store in brood pots. If a female allocates a large quantity of nectar and pollen to one brood pot, the grub that lives there will be able to grow large. If the pot is stingily provisioned, the larva can do nothing about it and is destined to become a small adult.

The problem for female bees is how to allocate their lifetime collection of brood provisions so as to maximize their reproductive success. In theory, it would be possible for a female to gain more descendants by producing a gang of small sons, rather than by investing a great deal in one or two much beefier sons. It is the sum of the reproductive achievements of all her sons, not the success of any one individual, that determines how many descendants she ultimately will have.

In any event, it is clear that females relatively rarely create large sons; instead they usually provision for medium or small males. These individuals emerge into a social environment dominated by the relatively few but extremely powerful large males. Although smaller males cannot eliminate the reproductive differential between them and the big battlers, they do some things that probably reduce the deficit. For example, small bees are rarely found in the bundles of males rolling on the ground in a furious fight for a female. Smaller digger bees apparently either learn or somehow are programmed to avoid these struggles, which they are most unlikely to win. Instead, they keep searching for a digging site where they might be lucky enough to excavate a female without interruption from a bigger rival.

Many small males keep away from larger males altogether by not patrolling emergence areas in search of digging sites. They hover, instead, poised in the air by mesquite trees or flowering palo verdes on the periphery of an emergence area. Hoverers distribute themselves evenly about their station and rush after any object that flies overhead, sprinting with equal conviction after a little stone thrown by a manipulative human observer, a passing bee (male or female), even a bird that happens to be flying from one mesquite to the next.

The hovering tactic may yield an occasional mating for small males; hoverers can pursue and capture rare flying virgin females that have emerged on their own or that have escaped from digger males without being mated, as sometimes happens when a digger is attacked just as the female scrabbles to the surface. Because small males are such poor fighters they do not have to reap a large reproductive return from their hovering mating tactic in order to do better than they would by trying to battle larger digger bees on their terms.

The behavioral flexibility of digger bees, like their capacity to find virgins they cannot see, is not unique to their species. Intense social competition is common among male insects, and individuals that are losing or would lose in the main avenue of competition often do something else, "making the best of a bad job" in the words of Richard Dawkins of Oxford University. You will recall that some male cactus flies control oviposition sites needed by their females and that these males are always permitted to mate by the females that come to these locations to lay their eggs. Males excluded from this high return tactic still try to mate, with indifferent but occasional success, by pursuing females in places like the sheltering crevices in a fallen saguaro. The ability to adopt one of several options, picking the tactic that maximizes an individual's mating chances in its social environment, given its body size and fighting ability, is the kind of thing that has evolved repeatedly in insects, belying their image as automatons.

Even if digger bees were complete automatons, most people still would consider them exceedingly skillful and entertaining ones. Thanks to the action of Darwinian selection, each individual has the unconscious goal of trying to reproduce more than any other member of its species, a goal that sets the males frantically digging, wrestling, tumbling, hovering, and darting about so quickly that they do not always look where they are going. After a month or five weeks, when the emergence area is occupied by the last males of the season, buzzing about slowly on tattered wings, the place seems subdued, on hold until the melodrama resumes the next spring, bringing noisy violence, sex, and excitement once again to a mesquite forest by a desert river.

May Twilight

I n the late afternoon the desert seems exhausted, all life drained by the exertion of coping with another savage day. The air crackles with dryness; the humidity stands at less than ten percent. Heat has clarified the land, leaving absolute stillness in the shaded, east-facing slope of Usery Mountain.

A distant cicada bursts into a metallic whine that builds in intensity and then stops, truncated in midsentence, as if the insect had suddenly realized how inappropriate its noisy signal is for the time and place. A melancholy silence resumes its grip on the mountainside. The shadows build gradually on the darkness they have already formed.

But up at the top of the mountain a slight breeze pushes over the saddle; the descending sun, although muted somewhat, still holds court. Five white-winged doves rush over the ridge, wings pounding in the urgent manner of doves, bodies turning slightly as they hurtle toward a last-minute destination.

In the lee of the saddle a family of ash-throated flycatchers perches in a palo verde. They engage in a subdued throaty chatter before tumbling out of the tree one by one, to alight in nearby jojobas and other shrubs.

In a patch of creosote bush between the two peaks of Usery Mountain an orange bee hovers, a huge bee whose wings blur in flight as the insect drifts up, then to one side, loops out, then back. Another orange bee stations himself in a creosote lower on the saddle, and another occupies a hovering site in the crown of a palo verde growing on the peaktop itself. Their faint droning flight runs on and on. A sweet floral scent drifts downwind from each insect.

The sun dips closer and closer to the horizon west of Phoenix. The Salt River becomes a great silvery reflector, shimmering with low-angled light.

A bee swings out widely from its creosote marker, comes back, races out again, and zooms along the ridge, quickly disappearing from view.

The day grows more somber still. A turkey vulture rides the slight updraft from the breeze striking the west-facing mountainside. The shadows on the other side of the mountain now sweep nearly to the top of lesser neighboring peaks.

The second and third bees swoop out from their hovering stations and depart just as the sun drops to touch the skyscrapers in distant downtown Phoenix.

Twilight.

In the sweep of flat land to the south and west, occupied by Mesa, Tempe, and Phoenix, lights begin to appear as dots across the valley. They glow like incandescent coals in the vague interim between the brilliant day and the charcoal night.

Hands Off the Gila Monster!

A small excavation pit in the gravel and clay of the hillside shows where a consumer of purplish broom-rapes has been at work under a scraggly bursage. A coyote scat lies in the trail nearby; bleached rib bones of the mouse or woodrat that fed the coyote poke through the tangle of hairs. One black fly perches on the clean, white, heat-dried scat.

A gila monster lurches past the coyote sign, then startles and tumbles downhill with ungainly twists of its body. It stops and looks slowly about, trying to trace the source of its uneasiness. Gila monsters do not appear to be the intellectuals of the desert world. After a pause to recover its composure, it begins to amble slowly forward, its orange-red and black beaded body weaving slowly among the bursages. The plump eighteen-inch-long lizard pulls itself up into a brittlebush and morosely turns its broad head from side to side as if attempting to remember what it was looking for. In the dappled shade of the shrub its black and red blotches are no longer conspicuous, but merge with the irregular patches of filtered sunlight and shade. The gila monster slides down and out of the plant and emerges on the other side, once again a complete lizard out in the open, swinging its brilliantly patterned body over the bare ground toward another shrub.

From the perspective of most, gila monsters (*Heloderma suspectum*) are worthy of note primarily because they are the only venomous lizards in the world, save one other closely related species, the Mexican beaded lizard, whose Latin name, *Heloderma horridum*, accurately reflects the usual attitude toward any animal that can defend itself — even to a small degree — against humans. The gila monster's lower jaw possesses a pair of poison glands, each connected to a grooved fang along which the venom can travel when the lizard has grasped a prey (or a human hand) in its substantial mouth.

The toxicity of their venom and the risk posed by gila monsters to human welfare often have been overstated, even to the point of absurdity. H. R. Moore, in his 1959 article on the lizard in *Arizona Days and Ways* magazine, claimed that a single drop of gila monster venom placed on desert soil would permanently kill all vegetation within a radius of ten yards. Moreover, in a kind of Chernobyl

A gila monster rests in the filtered shade of a palo verde.

effect, all animals that stumbled into the contaminated area for months afterward also were supposed to die, leaving their skeletons as silent testimony to the extreme danger of gila monsters. Here is a world-class tall tale, a real whopper, testimony both to H. R. Moore's vivid imagination and to the gullibility of the editorial board of *Arizona Days and Ways* in 1959.

It is true that occasionally someone is unfortunate enough to experience the bulldog clamp of a gila monster's bite. Dr. Findlay Russell, a thoroughly reputable observer, reports that he once treated a motorcyclist whose vehicle left the road and crashed into a dry wash. As the tumbling cyclist tried to break his fall he inserted his hand into the mouth of a gila monster, who happened to be in the wrong place at the wrong time as far as both the extraordinarily unlucky man and lizard were concerned. Most human injuries caused by gila monsters (and by rattlesnakes, for that matter) occur when a captive specimen is mishandled by its captor. Robert L. Smith of the University of Arizona warns that a person who finds his hand in the viselike grip of a tenacious gila monster may well have to pry the animal's jaws apart with a stick to regain control of his hand. This vivid advice suggests that it is best not to fondle gila monsters.

Gila monsters rarely exercise their venomous bite on humans; usually they save their toxins for their principal prey, small nestling birds and baby woodrats and rabbits. When foraging, the lizards typically wander long distances, poking their broad heads into bursages and brittlebushes, as well as inspecting woodrat nests and rabbit burrows. Should a gila monster discover a black-throated sparrow's nest in a desert plant, it will methodically consume the eggs or nestlings and then move on. In fact, bird eggs appear to be a primary source of nutrition for the lizard, and it need not envenomate prey in this category. If a gila monster sniffs out a den containing a clutch of baby rabbits, it has the capacity to consume them all. (Daniel Beck of the University of Arizona dispassionately watched a gila monster down four helpless bunnies in a row, a four-course meal that weighed one-third as much as the lizard itself.)

In years of desert hiking I have encountered foraging gila monsters only infrequently. Thanks to the studies of Lauren Porzer, I know that my failure to spot the lizard probably does not stem from a lack of alertness on my part. Porzer required many hours of work over two years in order to capture a grand total of eight gila monsters. She searched for her subjects on foot and also buried open cans in the soil, with screening aligned to funnel wandering lizards into her traps. She took the gila monsters she captured to a laboratory and implanted small radio transmitters in their abdominal cavities. After the creatures had recovered from this minor surgery they were returned to the locations from which they had been taken. Porzer then used a portable receiver and hand-held antenna to pick up signals coming from the transmitters, thereby locating her animals precisely day after day.

From her radio-broadcasting specimens Porzer learned many useful things about gila monsters' natural history. First, gila monsters are largely inactive for nearly nine months of the year. Except for April, May and June, the lizards are likely to be resting quietly in an earthen burrow, doing absolutely nothing. Even during the late spring and early summer, when the animals occasionally ramble after bird eggs and baby quail, they still spend ninety-five percent of each day underground. The period of greatest activity occurs not at night, but in the morning between 7:30 and 9:00 A.M., although the animals sometimes take an early evening stroll as well.

Second, gila monsters have a home range, a familiar area in which they remain from year to year. In Porzer's study site, individuals stayed within areas ranging from 1.5 to more than 22 hectares (or roughly 4 to 55 acres). When they did move, the lizards sensibly tended to follow washes, taking the easy routes to dense vegetation rich in bird nests and rabbit warrens.

Gila monsters are, therefore, extreme specialists whose lives are tied to early summer food production in the Sonoran Desert. April, May, and June are the months when most desert birds and mammals try to reproduce, creating a brief pulse of resources that gila monsters can exploit in their reptilian manner. By July bird eggs and nestlings have disappeared, woodrat young have died or dispersed, and finding food must be extremely difficult for a lumbering gila monster. As a result, the lizards simply sit out the hard times in self-imposed exile, waiting until the return of the brief season when the dangers they risk and the energy they expend by going aboveground will be compensated by the regular discovery of food. They have to do well during their hunting time, because they face long months with little or nothing to eat in a withered desert, a challenging time best spent conserving energy, living off the fat extracted from bird eggs and stored in their expandable plump tails. The dormant gila monsters sprawl in their burrows, their beautiful red and black spotted torsos immobile, their black chins pressed to the dusty ground.

June

From a yellow-green Mormon tea dangles the cast white
cuticle of a walkingstick insect. The wind shakes the
scrubby shrub; the nearly weightless cuticle, left behind by
its owner after moulting, billows like a wind sock. A jackrabbit has snipped many of the leafless stems of the Mormon tea and left them lying dead on the ground, uneaten.

June is the month of almost no hope. In central Arizona
June brings an average of less than two-tenths of an inch of
rain, while the average daily high will be 102 degrees. It is
a time for hanging on, enduring, letting the days pass.

A fragment of cloud moves slowly to the east, carried by
a wind that has removed almost every hint of moisture
from the desert world.

The seedpods of foothills palo verdes have begun to drop
from the trees, dried and brown. The yellow flowers that
fell earlier to the ground have blown away and crumbled
into a debris too fine to see. The season of reproduction is
over for most desert plants, but the saguaros on the hillside
hold their flowers high, supporting what will be the salva-
tion of many animals in the hard days of midsummer, for
this is the month when saguaro flowers become rich, ripe
fruits.

From the boulders on the still-shaded lower slope of
Usery Mountain comes a song, the clear, descending trill of
a canyon wren. Loud, defiant and encouraging, it an-
nounces a survivor. A blur of chestnut brown and white,
the wren bounces from rock to rock at perfect ease in its
home in the desert.

Poorwill

The sand in the wash running down from the ridge is alive with the footprints of peccary and quail, although neither animal is in sight in the early morning. They have retired to thickets of hackberry, desert broom, and tomatillo, places where shade makes the June day bearable. Even now, a little past dawn, there is no question of summer's dominance.

A cast snake skin has caught in the shrub the snake used to pull its old covering off when the new one had developed. Perched by the skin is a large robberfly, which noisily buzzes off to another ambush site to wait for a passing insect immune to the heat but not to the predatory fly's sudden assault.

The little seep in the wash has been reduced to the smallest of puddles, the moist earth on its border disturbed by various night-time diggers and visitors. In the early morning a small army of honey bees already encircles the water, or what is left of it, greedily drinking what they can.

Up the hillside toward the ridgeline an ash-throated flycatcher glides from one palo verde to another. It gives a soft, economical note of alarm. The teddy-bear cholla shine as if they were illuminated from within, reflecting the pure light of morning from their radiant coats of creamy spines.

My ascent of the ridgeline begins; a rock slips under my foot. There has been no rain for eight weeks, and the desert plants seem brittle from the long wait.

A poorwill flushes from a little cavity in the desiccated hillside, slipping downslope with a mothlike flurry of wings to settle abruptly on the ground out of view. This is the third year in which a poorwill has used this nest site. Last year at this time there were two white eggs gleaming in the darkness of the nest chamber, which is about the size of a shoebox. Today the "nest" is empty.

Is this the same poorwill that was here a year ago and a year before that? Many birds, even highly migratory species, are faithful to the same nesting location year after year. Several researchers have found that individuals return to the same spot if they succeeded in rearing young there the preceding breeding season. They shift nesting locations if the previous season was a disaster. This seems sensible enough. And the poorwill's nest cavity appears to be a perfect spot in which to rear a youngster or two; it is marvelously inconspicuous, sheltered from the sun and from the gaze of predators. I would never have spotted the nest site in the first place had I not all but stepped on it in the course of going up the ridge. It is possible, therefore, that the poorwill that found this spot has had success and has returned to it regularly.

On the other hand, it is just as likely that such a good location is attractive to many poorwills. If one year's owners die, other birds may come to occupy the spot in subsequent years. The only way to determine the correct scenario is to capture and mark the residents one year and check again the next. This would be a difficult job, and one that has yet to be accomplished, leaving me free to entertain the hope that the same poorwills have nested successfully three years running in this small niche in the desert.

The fact that poorwills do not construct a nest bowl of any sort stems from their ancestry. They, like the lesser nighthawk, are goatsuckers or caprimulgids, and all members of this family of birds simply deposit their eggs on the ground. When the adult bird is incubating throughout the day, its beautifully camouflaged plumage of brown, black, and tan flecked with white keeps the eggs relatively safe. Poorwills possess the color pattern typical of goatsuckers, as well as the habit of sitting tight as a predator approaches, popping up only at absolutely the last minute. Many coyotes and people have surely come within a few feet of nesting poorwills without realizing it.

Poorwills differ from lesser nighthawks in a number of ways. They are smaller birds, with soft, rounded wings rather than the long, angular wings of coursing nighthawks. Unlike the nighthawks, which race through the sky at dawn and dusk after agile flying insects, the poorwill is much more nocturnal and apparently does not so much chase its prey down as surprise it in near darkness.

Is the greater nocturnality of poorwills linked to the fact that their eggs are an unblemished white or pale pink, rather than the highly mottled grey, white, and brown of the eggs of lesser nighthawks? Because nighthawks often hunt insects in the early evening and late morning, they must leave their eggs untended when it is still light enough for various predators to see them lying on the ground. This circumstance would favor camouflaged eggs, and those of the nighthawk clearly qualify as cryptic. In contrast, the eggs of poorwills are extremely conspicuous because they lack the grey stippling, brown blotches and Jackson Pollack doodles found on lesser nighthawk eggs. But poorwills sit on their eggs the whole day long, a fact that may make camouflaged eggshells superfluous (just as the eggs of birds that nest in tree holes are white because they are out of view of visually hunting predators).

If the hypothesis that eggshell camouflage is a function of the probability that eggs will be left uncovered during daylight hours, then one would expect whip-poor-wills and chuck-wills-widows to have uncamouflaged eggs, because these birds, like poorwills, are active primarily at night. A check of the *Field Guide to the Nests, Eggs and Nestlings of North American Birds* left me feeling uncertain about the validity of my hypothesis. It is clear from the egg descriptions and illustrations in the text that the two most day-active goatsuckers, the two North American nighthawks, have the most highly marked, camouflaged eggs of any of our caprimulgids; the poorwill is the only species to have pure white or unmarked whitish eggs. The other goatsuckers evidently are intermediate, having eggs that are sparsely marked but nevertheless lightly blotched. If my hypothesis is to be rescued, it would be necessary to show that poorwills are less likely to leave their eggs during the day than are whip-poor-wills and their other caprimulgid cousins. Certainly something odd is going on here, because almost all birds that nest on the ground or in the open have cryptically colored eggs. Why the poorwill is an exception needs some explanation.

The extreme camouflage afforded by poorwill plumage may play a role in the bird's capacity to survive prolonged dormancy, as well as in the evolution of the color of its eggs. Some poorwills spend the chilly winter months in the deserts of western North America in a dormant state, during which time they sit absolutely still on a rocky ledge, eyes closed and body temperature reduced to about half that of an active bird. With their metabolism at half speed, they are able to survive cold weather and a lack of food for up to three months. But while they are dormant they cannot possibly detect, let alone escape from, a predator that spots them. Nevertheless, predators may have a difficult time finding a helpless "hibernating" poorwill because of its immobility and extraordinarily effective camouflage.

Thus there is a similarity of sorts between gila monsters and poorwills, in that both species face long periods in the Sonoran Desert when there simply is not enough for them to eat. In the face of this cold truth, the lizard and the poorwill hunker down for the

A poorwill relies on camouflage to protect it from its enemies.

duration, minimizing their metabolic expenditures during the hard times, enabling some to survive to exploit what are for them the productive seasons in their spartan world.

The poorwill on Usery Ridge flutters into the air again and flies further downhill, alighting on a flat-topped boulder painted with black desert varnish. The pale grey stems of brittlebush surround the boulder. The beautiful bird has settled snugly into a little depression on the rock as if it were nesting there. It sits tight, not moving, its eyes the narrowest of slits. The poorwill turns to stone and becomes the desert.

How to Wave to a Predator — and Get Away with It

Silence envelopes the sandy wash. Verdins and gnatcatchers have nothing to say this morning. The air is so dry and so still that it is as if the atmosphere itself has evaporated.

But not every animal has disappeared. A white-winged dove flies over the lip of the ridge bordering the wash and banks sharply. The rhythm of its wingbeats changes as it hurtles eastward. A late empress butterfly male leaves its perch, a twig elevated above the overheated sand by a hackberry tree, and sails rapidly out and back to his perch again. He is one of the last of his tribe this season.

A zebra-tailed lizard, which had been crouched in the pale gravel of the dry wash, bursts into a madcap dash down the streambed. The lizard possesses a delicate off-white color pattern that melts into the background of the wash when the animal is still. At the end of its brief Olympic sprint it stops suddenly, almost disappearing, except that it curls the tip of its long and elegant tail upward and waves it back and forth like a military signalman. The black bands that circle the waving tail give the lizard its common name and make the animal dramatically conspicuous during its display.

Why should such a generally well-camouflaged creature as the zebra-tailed lizard go out of its way to flag its location upon the approach of a human from whom it appears to be trying to escape? When its tail is held flat against the ground the zebra stripes are not obvious and the lizard is all but invisible. It is only when the lizard raises its tail and twitches it from side to side that the creature all but jumps out of its surroundings.

Zebra-tailed lizards are not the only animals to wave a brightly marked body part when they confront a potential predator. The most familiar example of this phenomenon to North Americans is the tail-flagging of white-tailed deer; these animals often raise their tails, exposing the bright white underside, when fleeing in alarm from an approaching human, dog, or other enemy. Or consider the eastern swamphen, an Australian gallinule, that responds with tail flicks when a human walks toward it. As the bird rapidly raises and lowers its tail it exposes and then conceals its white rump patch.

A zebra-tailed lizard waves the conspicuously banded underside of its tail.

The flashes of white produced by tail-flicking irresistibly draw attention to the bird.

There has been a long debate on the function of flagging and flash colors of the sort exhibited by zebra-tailed lizards, white-tailed deer, and swamphens, a debate that illustrates how many different explanations can be advanced to account for an intriguing behavior. For example, perhaps tail waving spread through ancestral populations of the zebra-tailed lizard because an alarmed lizard could warn others of approaching danger, thereby helping maintain the species in its unending war with predators. We can call this the group-benefit hypothesis.

Hypotheses of this sort were once popular in biology and still linger on in places, although they are much less widely accepted than they once were. The problem with group-benefit or species-preservation hypotheses was only recognized in the mid-1960s when a few evolutionary biologists, prominently George C. Williams of the State University of New York at Stony Brook, offered critiques of the book *Animal Dispersion in Relation to Social Behaviour* by V. C. Wynne-Edwards. Wynne-Edwards proposed that populations or species composed of individuals that behaved in ways that promoted group survival would outlive those competing populations or species that lacked individuals willing or able to sacrifice themselves for the welfare of the group. Thus attributes that helped the group at the expense of individual survival and reproductive success were maintained, according to Wynne-Edwards's scheme, by *group selection*, in which the differential survival of groups determined the hereditary attributes passed on from generation to generation.

Wynne-Edwards attributed the evolution of flash colors and flagging behavior to group selection's favoring signals that helped keep a group of animals together in the face of danger. By this token, perhaps zebra-tailed lizards employ their tail semaphore code to alert others to the appearance of deadly enemies. Failing to offer the danger signal, according to the group selectionist approach, would contribute to a decline in the numbers of their species, thus weakening it and increasing the odds that it could become extinct.

Williams and others, however, pointed out a major defect in the theoretical underpinning of group-benefit hypotheses. Imagine a population whose members really were predisposed to give an alarm upon spotting a predator, an alarm that benefitted others but exposed the signal-giver to the cold-hearted attention of a predator. Imagine further that in such a population of self-sacrificing types there arose, by chance mutation, another kind of individual. This lizard made use of the warnings provided by others but did not risk tail-waving when it detected a predator; instead it took the personally safer route of keeping its tail flat on the ground after speeding away from a dangerous enemy. Surely in such a population a "selfish" type would reproduce more successfully than "altruistic" types. From one generation to the next, the genes that promoted self-preservation would spread at the expense of the genes that advanced group survival.

Williams concluded that indiscriminate assistance of the sort required by most group-benefit hypotheses would be selected *against* by the stronger force of selection acting at the level of individuals. He felt, and almost every biologist now agrees, that hypotheses that assume or demand that individuals do not promote the spread of their own genes but instead act for the benefit of all members of their group are unlikely to be correct. Instead, he suggested that biologists really ought to ask how apparently helpful acts might serve the selfish reproductive interests of the individual that engages in them.

Many biologists were quick to take Williams's suggestion, and well they might in the case of zebra-tailed lizards, which are not social animals. The fact that zebra-tails do not roam Sonoran Desert washes in small bands, but instead lead solitary lives, greatly decreases the attractiveness of any hypothesis holding that tail-waving is a social signal designed to benefit another individual.

One cannot so readily dismiss a social function for the flash signals of other species that *do* live in groups. For such species we might wish to consider the possibility that the signal selectively aids the offspring of the signaler or relatives of the signaler, two categories of individuals that share genes in common with the warning-giver. By helping its relatives survive, an animal could actually increase the frequency of the genes responsible for its helpful behavior.

In the case of zebra-tailed lizards, is it possible that tail-waving serves "selfish" ends by helping the signaling lizard survive, despite what superficially appears to be suicidal behavior? The biologist N. Smythe has argued that tail-waving is indeed reproductively advantageous for the waver. His pursuit-invitation hypothesis states that by flagging or flashing a body part a prey species makes itself more conspicuous to a predator, but not to encourage the predator to capture it. Instead, the essence of pursuit-invitation is that the prey makes itself conspicuous and attractive to induce a hungry predator to "show its hand" by chasing the signaling prey.

This ingenious hypothesis is based on two key assumptions. First, it assumes that prey will try to induce chasing only when there is an excellent chance of escape. Second, the hypothesis assumes that by getting a predator to reveal its intentions, prey animals can save time and energy they would otherwise expend trying to avoid or keep track of predators that really are not interested in hunting them. For example, satiated predators usually will not try to capture and kill still more victims. By inviting attack, an animal can quickly determine whether a particular predator is worth worrying about or whether it is safe to feed or rest, rather than remain on high alert, while the predator is nearby.

Although it was a splendid idea, the pursuit-invitation hypothesis was not immune to criticism. Several skeptics argued that if it were true that prey gave the flash signal only when it was safe to do so, then over evolutionary time predators would come to ignore the invitation to pursue these animals. Imagine two types of individuals in the predator population. One type is a sucker for the invitation signal and spends considerable cumulative effort running after prey that cannot be captured. The other type stops hunting if it sees a potential victim signal, because the odds of a successful chase are stacked heavily in favor of the prey under these circumstances. Discriminating predators surely would conserve more time and energy than would those that dashed off to accept every pursuit invitation they received.

This analysis, founded in the logic of selectionist thinking, yields an alternative explanation for tail-waving, the pursuit-deterrence hypothesis. The idea is similar to the pursuit-invitation argument, in that both suggest that the function of a prey's flash or flagging signal is to communicate with a predator. But the pursuit-deterrence hypothesis assumes that it may be in the self-interest of predators to ignore prey that alertly signal "I have seen you," because such prey are all but impossible to catch. It also is in the self-interest of prey to announce that they have seen a predator if this ends the enemy's attempt to catch them, saving them valuable time and energy. Thus both parties can benefit, and so the prey's signal and the predator's response to it can persist over evolutionary time even if a mutant prey individual should arise, one that does not give the signal, or a mutant predator should appear that does not stop its hunt when prey announce that they have seen the predator.

No one has attempted to test any hypothesis on tail-waving by zebra-tailed lizards, a point that illustrates how much easier it is to devise possible explanations than to determine which is likely to be right. In theory, however, tests could be developed for any of the above hypotheses. For example, a simple prediction from the pursuit-invitation hypothesis is that natural predators of the lizard will be more prone to chase tail-waving individuals than to chase those that keep their tails pressed flat to the soil; the pursuit-deterrence hypothesis generates exactly the opposite prediction. We therefore have a way of discriminating clearly between competing ideas, although observing a sufficient number of predator-prey interactions to establish which prediction is correct would be all but impossible in the field. Perhaps the simplest test would involve the experimental introduction of a number of zebra-tails into an enclosure with a lizard-eating predator, perhaps a snake. By attending to the responses of the captive predator to lizards that did and did not wave their tails, an experimenter could perhaps determine whether the lizards' behavior stimulated attacks or discouraged them.

Until these or other tests are done, the function of tail-waving by zebra-tailed lizards will remain unknown, but the animals can be enjoyed nonetheless. They are a wonderful part of Sonoran Desert summer days because they provide explosive motion and surprise when they scuttle down a wash, parting the bone-dry air and raising their tails to wave cheekily at their observers.

Altruism Among Ground Squirrels

As a general rule, I do not interfere with the natural course of events affecting the animals I observe. One exception came when I rescued a small male wasp from a spider's web. I knew the male well, having marked him with a dab of paint and having studied his behavior on his mating territory for several days before he blundered into a spider's web. Rather than lose him and have to start over with a new male, I snatched him away from the approaching spider and certain death and returned him to his domain in one piece. If he was grateful to me, he did not show it.

Another rare mission of mercy occurred some years ago when I saw a large gopher snake with his head in a round-tailed ground squirrel burrow and three small, furry youngsters standing (terrified?) at the entrance. I pulled the snake back firmly. Not surprisingly, the irritated reptile struck at me. I promptly released the snake, which slithered hastily away, no doubt to find another batch of vulnerable ground squirrel infants at another burrow.

My desire to intervene was triggered by the extraordinarily appealing appearance of baby round-tailed ground squirrels. Now, in early June, the baby round-tails are beginning to grow out of their cartoon cuteness, but they are still ridiculously attractive animals. Even the adults are pleasant to watch, but when the babies first venture out of their mother's burrow in the sandy floodplain of the Salt River they could easily be mistaken for a creation of Walt Disney. Big-headed, with huge, moist eyes, they totter about on tiny legs, stimulating warm protective feelings in all but the most hardhearted human. They seem remarkably tame and unalert, given the host of enemies in their neighborhoods. If Cooper's hawks and gopher snakes could salivate, I am sure they would when a young round-tailed ground squirrel wobbled into view.

Round-tailed ground squirrels, however, are not as much at the mercy of their predators as they might appear. For one thing, adult squirrels give distinctive alarm calls when they spot a potential predator, such as a human or a coyote. These squeaky screeches send all nearby foraging squirrels, young and old alike, dashing back to the relative safety of their tunnels.

The squeaky alarm callers seem to be helping others with their alarms, but are they? Just as in the case of tail-waving by zebratailed lizards, this is a tricky question because there are so many possible functions for the signal. For example, it could be that the primary function of the squeak is to tell an enemy that the squeaker has seen it and that the predator, therefore, would be well advised to hunt for a less alert, easier-to-catch victim. That other squirrels react to the call could be an incidental effect, as these animals simply take advantage of the signal for their own purposes and not because it is in the caller's interests to warn them. On the other hand, alerting others could indeed be the evolved function of the alarm call, with the signaler giving its call specifically to assist others. For example, a squeaking ground squirrel might gain by warning its babies that an enemy is near, encouraging them to get back to their burrow, even though giving the call might be risky if it draws the attention of the hunter to the caller.

In order to discriminate among these and a number of other hypotheses, it helps to know a few things. First, does giving an alarm call really put the caller at greater risk of attack? Knowing the answer to this question would tell us whether the function of the signal is to improve the survival of the caller itself or, perhaps, to help others stay alive. The best-studied case of alarm-calling in ground squirrels is the work done with Belding's ground squirrel, a species found in the Sierra Nevadas of California, where Paul Sherman of Cornell University and his many assistants have spent years tracking down the significance of this behavior. Sherman demonstrated that for Belding's ground squirrel, giving an alarm signal on detecting a coyote or badger is costly to the signaler, who is then much more likely to be chased down and killed than are the individuals that react to the call.

Sherman also discovered that the Belding's ground squirrels that give alarm calls tend to be females, not males. Because he had marked large numbers of individuals, Sherman knew what he needed to know about the social organization of Belding's ground squirrels in order to make sense of this result. This species is one in which males search widely, mating with as many females as they can before they move on, leaving their mates behind to rear their young on their own. As a result, when a female takes a risk to sound the alarm her youngsters may be able to benefit from it. Their improved survival enhances the female's chances of leaving descendants, thereby providing the evolutionary basis for alarm-call-giving by *females*. A male that gives a warning is likely to be far from his offspring, and so he gets nothing back for his costly helpfulness. The decreased chance of survival for alarm-calling males creates selection against this behavior in *males*.

But Sherman found that females *without* young also were willing to give self-sacrificing alarm calls. Thus the behavior cannot be explained solely in terms of productive parental care. Females without infants might give alarm signals because the squirrels form matriarchal neighborhoods with their mothers, sisters, aunts, and nieces. The fact that a female lives within a kind of unisex extended family means that an alarm-caller can benefit close female relatives other than her own offspring.

Because related animals share genes in common by virtue of having a common ancestor, helping a relative stay alive helps keep some fraction of your genes alive as well. A parent has only half its genes in each offspring (the other half coming from the parent's mate). Ultimately, the significance of parental care is to promote the survival of the genes a parent shares with the offspring it helps.

Young ground squirrels with their mother at the entrance to their nest burrow.

Helping a niece or sister thwart a predator has essentially the same end result as protecting one's infant. To the extent that alarm-calling really helps, the genetic basis for the trait can be promoted when the beneficiaries are kin of all types.

Sherman's explanation for certain kinds of alarm-calling by female Belding's ground squirrels is that the action helps offspring and near relatives of the self-sacrificing alarm-giver. Males do not call because they are unlikely to aid either their progeny or other relatives, given their pattern of dispersal after the mating season.

We can test Sherman's hypothesis by finding a species in which males remain near enough to their relatives to be in a position to help them. We would predict that males of such a species will give alarm calls as often as females, because both sexes can advance their genetic contribution to the next generation by keeping their youngsters alive in a world filled with hawks, snakes, and coyotes.

While at the University of Arizona, Christopher Dunford conducted the same kind of study of round-tailed ground squirrels that Sherman had done on Belding's ground squirrels. Dunford marked a large number of individuals and learned about their patterns of residency and dispersal; he found that after the mating season, adult male round-tails head for the next county just like male Belding's ground squirrels. Dunford also monitored who was giving alarm calls and who was keeping quiet, and here, too, there was no difference between the two species, since male round-tails also usually remain silent in the face of danger.

Juvenile males, however, spend the summer with their mothers and siblings. They are nearby when their siblings are growing up, instead of living hundreds of meters away in the company of genetic strangers. They are just as likely to sound the alarm as are females of their species, proving that there is nothing inherently nasty about male ground squirrels. Their behavior has evolved in a variety of social contexts, and when it is genetically advantageous to promote the welfare of others, males do give warning signals.

By the same token, the behavior of female ground squirrels is most definitely not indiscriminately self-sacrificing and unselfish. Females are helpful when these actions tend to advance the welfare of their particular genes. When a female Belding's ground squirrel encounters a nonrelative she is likely to respond in a most ungentlewomanly fashion, chasing the other female away or even sneaking into her nest burrow to kill her youngsters, having put all parental kindness and sisterly emotions utterly aside.

An evolutionary dissection of the behavior of ground squirrels makes it a bit more difficult to view them sentimentally, knowing that self-interest dominates their behavior as much as it does our own. On the other hand, it is a beautiful thing in its own right that female squirrels have the special abilities that enable them to act effectively on behalf of their relatives. And a June without baby round-tails cavorting among dried grasses in the filtered shade of a blue palo verde or a creosote bush would be a diminished June and an incomplete summer.

June's Saguaro

On a bleached hillside a saguaro sticks four fat fingers rudely in the air. Diamonds of white glitter from two fingertips; the other two sport immature green fruit and blackened twists of tissue where flowers once were. The remaining flowers are magnificent creations. A big ring of waxy white petals surrounds a central mass of yellow-orange stamens, which in turn encircle a carpel. The carpel's stigma thrusts out well past the pollen-laden stamens, a design that helps prevent self-pollination. Instead, when a bat comes visiting at night and thrusts its face into the flower, pollen from other flowers that have been caught on the bat's furry jaws will be brushed onto the stigma.

At the junction of two fingers and the main trunk a red-tailed hawk has built a giant nest, one twig at a time. The guano-bespattered mound of palo verde branches and creosote limbs is topped by two infant red-tails, each about to fledge but still tufted with white down. An adult bird circles anxiously overhead, calling "kee-yer" repetitiously. The panting youngsters crouch down while honey bees hover by the glorious flowers far above them.

The totem saguaros, squat jojobas and feathery palo verdes are about all that remains green in an environment now monopolized by pale browns and greys. The pads of prickly pears look pinched and shrunken. Cactus wrens slip furtively among the chollas.

Range Wars

The rocky outcrops high on Usery Peak look out over a small army of saguaros standing immobile on the slope below the peak. A late-season male tarantula hawk perches on one giant saguaro that pokes up higher than all the rest. The wasp sallies out after another tarantula hawk male, one of only a handful of rivals that pass by during my hourlong watch. Males of these insects defend prominent cacti and palo verdes growing on mountain ridges and peaks. From their vantage points they wait with immense patience for the arrival of females, while chasing other males away. It is always a long wait; the territories protected by males have nothing in the way of nectar or spider prey or potential nest sites that would attract females interested in finding valuable food or nest burrows. Instead, the territories serve merely as landmarks from which males can scan for incoming females intent on mating. With copulation completed, a female wastes no time in departing for other areas that contain food and places in which to nest. Her partner remains behind, ticking off the hours of vigil until the next female sails in to receive a donation of sperm in a minute's mating.

The tarantula hawk's saguaro territory is one in a cluster of cacti with relatively exuberant blooms, and from time to time the wasp briefly inspects a black-chinned hummingbird that is also stationed on a cactus, from which it darts out to visit flowers on various other saguaros growing nearby.

The hummingbird sits on the glossy petals of a flower and sticks its head deep into the cup-shaped blossom to drink the nectar within. It ignores the tarantula hawk that buzzes past on frayed wings. But when another hummingbird comes whistling in — with great bravado — the feeding bird instantly abandons its perch and darts after the newcomer in a flurry of twists and dives. As the hummers swoop up and down above the contested saguaro they scold each other with a scratchy run of chips until the dogfight ends with the departure of one of the birds. The winner (and I am unable to determine whether it is the original nectar-consumer or the newcomer) returns to feed on saguaro ambrosia at intervals, while interacting with a series of invaders who attempt (perhaps successfully) to overthrow it in an unceasing competition to claim control of the patch of blooms.

Two black-chinned hummingbirds engage in aerial combat over a feeding territory centered on the flowers of a saguaro.

The hummingbird's territoriality is very different from the tarantula hawk wasp's site defense. The bird's readiness to fight for saguaros occurs because heavily flowering cacti offer concentrated food resources. Nectar-feeding birds often battle for feeding sites, a trait exhibited by American hummingbirds, Australian honeyeaters, Hawaiian honeycreepers, and African sunbirds, among others. Because these birds are conspicuous, attractive, and fun to watch, they have been the subjects of any number of research projects designed to analyze the economics of resource-based territoriality. These projects have revealed that individual birds are remarkably sensitive to the energetic costs and benefits of trying to defend a particular source of nectar. A honeycreeper or honeyeater does not invest in territorial defense just for the pleasure of possession. When the gains in terms of nectar energy to be taken from the site are less than the energetic expenses associated with defending it, the birds either stop being territorial or at least reduce their time and energy investment in aggression. No knee-jerk aggressiveness for them; they want a payoff, and they somehow know when fighting is counterproductive.

The sophistication of the assessment abilities of territorial nectar-feeders has been explored in a number of ways, including some devious experimental manipulations. For example, Paul Ewald of Amherst College took advantage of the well-known enthusiasm of hummingbirds for sugar-water feeders, which they will avidly defend under appropriate circumstances. Ewald induced black-chinned hummingbirds to guard specially designed feeders capable of producing a precisely regulated flow of sucrose solution. He then forced birds at neighboring feeders to fight with one another by stringing a line between the two feeders and gradually moving them closer and closer, until one bird could monopolize both food sources. Ewald wanted to know whether the bird's prior experience with the energy value of the food supplied by its feeder would influence its decision to fight for both feeders when one was within a couple of meters or so of the other.

To answer this question, Ewald placed two "rich" feeders a short distance apart; when black-chinned hummingbirds had claimed each one, he replaced his generous feeders with one that yielded eight-tenths of a millilitre of sugary fluid per hour and another that gave six-tenths of a millilitre per hour. As he shifted the two feeders closer together, the two owners came into more and more frequent and intense conflict, until finally one hummer gave up the fight and fled, leaving the other in charge of both dispensers. The winner in thirteen of the seventeen contests was the individual that had initially owned the richer of the two feeders. Even though juvenile black-chins are generally at a disadvantage when dealing with adults, when the juveniles possessed the more valuable experimental feeder they defeated adult rivals. Although the difference in the productivity of the two food sources was modest, it was sufficient to affect the motivation of competing hummingbirds. Owners of the poorer feeder presumably judged that acquiring a second feeder would yield only a mediocre increment in the amount of sucrose solution available per hour. Owners of the richer feeder had more to gain by retaining their superior food source, especially if they judged that they would be doubling it by taking over a second superfeeder.

This experiment illustrates nicely that black-chinned humming-birds know precisely what they derive from owning a territory and that this information influences their readiness to fight to maintain (or expand) their holdings. The sensitivity of black-chins to the economic value of a territory has been documented in other simpler ways as well. Birds that own a dispenser that gives eight-tenths of a millilitre of sugar water per hour spend more time by the feeder and more time chattering at and chasing intruders than do owners of slightly less productive feeders.

Black-chinned hummingbirds often vocalize in defense of their territories, and so the vigorous sparring battles over saguaro flowers are generally noisy. Paul Ewald and his coworker Raymond Bransfield documented that the richer the territory, the more likely black-chins are to supplement a chase with a chatter, perhaps to make the point as emphatically as possible that they are in charge here. Because black-chinned hummingbirds are small, even for hummingbirds, they are likely to be challenged by members of other, larger species. To the extent that their demonstration of a strong "determination" to defend a territory deters intruders of other species, black-chinned hummers may gain by announcing via chatters that a takeover attempt will at least be expensive.

At this time of year in the Sonoran Desert, black-chinned hummingbirds have only each other to contend with, and they make the most of it. Two rivals for saguaro ambrosia rush at each other, parrying and thrusting with their dagger-like bills, exhibiting an agility in a three-dimensional duel that would be the envy of the most accomplished human fencers. As the hummers dance through their combat, a trio of thick-billed house finches flutter clumsily down on ordinary wings to land atop a saguaro downslope. There they feed casually together, pushing their blunt heads into the open flowers while the hummingbirds chitter and squeak in their hot-blooded struggle, fashioning an aerial ballet based on cold-blooded economics.

The Hard Lives and Hard Times of Brittlebush

From a distance, one of the saguaros on the mountain appears to have sustained multiple flesh wounds; crimson splotches mark its limb tips. Closer inspection reveals that this cactus now has ripened fruit and that some have split open, exposing the brilliant red interior flesh and central mass of black seeds. These scarlet signals announce the beginning of a season of abundance for white-winged doves and a small army of other animals, all of which feast on mature saguaro fruits and seeds. Well they might; at sixteen percent protein and about twenty-five hundred calories per pound, saguaro seeds are a first-rate food.

The size and opulence of saguaros diminishes further the smaller plants that stand around them. Among the most abundant of these lesser species is the grey brittlebush. These plants in June are remarkably different from the brittlebushes of January. In mid-winter the little perennial shrubs are covered with large, green leaves—real leaves. Today the withered plants bear small scraps of pale dun tissue, twisted and curled—barely leaves at all. There is no excess flesh on these plants, nothing to spare for doves and woodrats, beetles and flies.

A little staghorn cactus hidden in an aestivating brittlebush waits (or so it seems) to impale passersby with its needle-tipped spines. It is a hard world. The brittlebushes have had no rain for months. The maximum daily temperature has been over 100 degrees for the past thirty days. The monsoon rains are not due for several weeks, and there is no guarantee that they will arrive on schedule.

Brittlebushes, like poorwills, are able to endure by becoming dormant when conditions are bad. The brittlebushes in the Usery Mountains gave up photosynthesis long ago by permitting their leaves to die. This put an end to the production of sugars, but it also ended the loss of water that accompanies the capture of carbon dioxide from the atmosphere by brittlebush leaves. Plant leaves are riddled with chambers that can be opened or closed. When the chambers are open, gas exchange occurs; carbon dioxide enters while water vapor is lost from the plant. Even when brittlebush maintains its photosynthetic equipment intact, it compromises gas

The desiccated leaves of a brittlebush begin to curl in the summer heat.

exchange by investing in a coat of fine hairs that cover each leaf. These help reflect burning sunlight and reduce water-losing transpiration, but they also lessen the leaves' effectiveness as carbon dioxide collectors.

Suburban brittlebush plants, which have suburban caretakers and suburban water in the summer, delay the production of hairs for their leaves, and they postpone complete leaf surgery, too, because they can afford to transpire. As a result, they continue to photosynthesize and to grow at times when in nature they would be aestivating. The typical desert brittlebush rarely exceeds two feet in height, but the brittlebush that I planted in my garden near the well-watered tangelo tree has become so abnormally large and leafy that it has lost its resemblance to real brittlebush. It is elephantine, mutant, almost disturbing in its dimensions. Offended by the garish thing I had created, I chopped the plant back severely, only to have it rebound with a compensatory burst of growth that made it once again a monstrosity in a remarkably short time.

In addition to the novel experience of irrigation, my brittlebush enjoys another advantage not available to its Sonoran Desert kin. It grows alone instead of in the company of other brittlebushes. Usually brittlebushes grow several feet apart. They might appear to be sufficiently separated to avoid interfering with each other, but because there is so little water in desert soil most of the year neighbors must compete for this limited commodity. Desert botanists have convincingly demonstrated how intense the competition is through the experimental removal of nearby plants from a sample of target bushes. These favored individuals flourished, freed from the struggle for water caused by proximity to others of their species. In one eighteen-month study, brittlebushes that had lost their nearest neighbors showed an increase in weight ten times greater than that of control plants left to contend with rivals for water. The experimental plants produced many more leaves and about three times as many flowers than did the controls. Thus brittlebushes that escaped from water shortages imposed by the root systems of nearby competitors turned their good fortune to reproductive advantage.

There are no obvious signs from the brittlebushes on a desert hillside that the plants are engaged in a fierce and nasty struggle with their neighbors. When you think about it, however, there are few differences between an aggregation of brittlebush plants and an aggregation of digger bees. In each group, individuals look out for number one. Their capacity to thwart other members of their species has just as much to say about how many descendants they will leave as does their ability to deal with predators and with the inanimate physical environment. Male digger bees unable to prevent other males from stealing their mates will leave few descendants. Brittlebushes unable to get at least as much water as their neighbors will flower poorly and set few seeds, leaving the evolutionary destiny of their species in the hands of those tough plants capable of winning the competition for water.

The brittlebushes in the Usery Mountains, although a wonderfully polished product of evolutionary competition, are unlikely to turn many heads in June. The thin, tan stalks that rise above the crumpled grey foliage and resin-dotted stems are the only hint that remains of the spring flowering season. Then these dried stalks had been green and supple, supports for a profusion of bright orange-yellow flowers. Today the brittlebushes fight for their lives, for a chance to see another spring, a time when water will be of less concern and when they can become transpiring Cinderellas for a flowery month before resuming a life of inconspicuous struggle.

Burn, Desert, Burn

I n late May of 1984 someone started a fire on the east-facing slope of a side ridge in the Usery Mountains. The fire ran up the hillside to the top of this ridge, blackening a ten-acre patch of desert. Luckily, a natural firebreak of sparse vegetation on the drainage line between the burned slope and the next kept the fire from spreading.

The early spring rains had promoted a dense crop of annuals that had dried under the early summer sun. The brittlebush had bloomed magnificently. The crisp tinder of desiccated plants fueled a fire hot enough to burn almost all the palo verdes and saguaros and jojobas on the slope. Here and there a survivor clung to the hillside, singed and maimed but alive.

On the ridge a short time after the fire a desolate odor of charcoal and dust hung in the air, but on the unburnt main ridge whiptail lizards and Gambel's quail went about their business unaffected.

Gradually the carnal scent of fire disappeared, but the burned area remained black and brown, apparently devoid of life, through the summer and into the fall. By the following spring, however, the hillside had undergone an extraordinary transformation. The fiddle-necks, normally a foot tall in the unburnt desert, grew twice as tall in the burn and in numbers that made the hillside look like a commercial flower garden. Deep orange poppies exploded wherever the fiddle-necks left space. They pushed up among the charcoal-black stems of dead jojobas, by the fire-cracked rocks on the hillside, near the burnt skeletons of *Opuntia* cacti. Other smaller annuals, with their less conspicuous but equally ornamental pink, white, and

Desert poppies grow on a burned patch of desert one year after a fire.

purple flowers, competed for growing sites on what had appeared until recently to be hopelessly barren soil.

The burn and the neighboring unburnt hillside might as well have been in two separate universes, the one exuberantly floral, the other stony and spartan, its barebones clumps of brittlebush and bursage accented by the occasional tuft of poppies or straggly fiddle-neck.

A mixed flock of black-throated and white-crowned sparrows played leapfrog as they moved down the hillside, gleaning seeds and insects among the cover of the annuals. A sparrow hawk angled back and forth, then hovered before plunging into the flowers after a grasshopper that had been feasting on the profusion of plants.

The spring show soon faded under the severe sun of May, and the hillside reverted to somber browns that gave little hint of the recent riot of annuals. The remains of densely packed annuals, however, gave the old burn a furry, woolly look quite unlike that of the unburned neighboring hillside, which was dominated by green perennial shrubs surrounded by expanses of bare ground.

In the spring of 1986 the vegetative pattern was repeated, although the annuals grew considerably less riotously. Some jojobas had resprouted from living rootstock and the slope became sparsely dotted with these little shrubs, complementing the few palo verdes and saguaros that had managed to make it through the fire.

With the passage of yet another year and the onset of a dry spring, the desert annuals gave 1987 a bye for the most part. In place of the native plants grew a rich stand of red brome grass, an import that grows abundantly enough on unaltered slopes, but which was largely absent from the devastated hillside the first year after the fire. The carpet of out-of-place red brome gave the old burn a dramatically different look from that of the surrounding areas in May 1987.

The casual little fire on the ridge clearly caused major changes in the ecology of the desert, a finding confirmed in studies conducted by George Cave, Duncan Patten, and Sam Loftin of Arizona State University at other Sonoran Desert burns. Although there may seem to be too little woody material in the desert to sustain a fierce, hot fire, there is, particularly by the end of the spring growing season. The little bursages and the mat of bone-dry grasses, cured in the kiln of late May, flame up quickly and intensely. Temperatures reach 400 degrees centigrade a little above the ground in a burning bursage patch. The fire consumes the bursage, kills the red brome grass seeds, kills the succulent cacti, rings the palo verdes, and eventually kills many of them, too. The oily jojobas crackle and burn down to their roots.

Happily, just two centimeters beneath the soil surface the temperature is only 60 degrees centigrade, a difference that permits the roots of some of the perennial shrubs (but not bursage) to survive. Although the cacti in the burn never regenerate, the jojobas and palo verdes may live to sprout again. Moreover, the fire releases compounds stored in plant tissues, raising levels of soil nitrogen available for plant growth for about a year, until new plants have used up the transient bonanza. There is little doubt that freed nitrogen was one of the reasons, perhaps the major reason, that the desert annuals did so well in the spring of 1985.

Moreover, fire removes competitors for nitrogen, space and water. With most perennials gone, there are more of these essential commodities for the survivors and for the annuals during their brief spring. Bursage seeds buried deeply enough in the soil to survive the fire have a field day in the absence of a battalion of mature competitors. Brittlebush seed blown in on the wind has a chance to get established in soils that have not been sucked dry by the shallow roots of saguaros and barrel cacti. Up pop seedlings of these species, quickly covering the open ground and probing for buried nitrates.

The old community will not reappear magically on the hillside any time soon, given the unforgiving removal of most of the slow-growing cacti that give the Sonoran Desert its essential character. Because the succulent cacti and palo verde show so little resilience in the face of fire, can fire have been common in the Sonoran Desert before modern civilization?

In those parts of the world where fire is a regular event in natural habitats, plants usually show signs of accommodating to the phenomenon, if not actually requiring it for full reproductive success. For example, the seeds of fire-frequented plants often must be cooked a little before they will deign to germinate. Certain eucalyptus trees in fire-swept parts of Australia can be completely defoliated and blackened from bottom to top by a stiff fire and yet still put out a new crop of leaves a short time later.

Although some Sonoran Desert plants do well in the spring after a burn, their success seems due more to the fertilizing effect of a fire than to any special adaptation for coping with wildfire itself. Wildfire may be something of a newcomer to the desert, linked directly and indirectly to human activity. Most fires in the desert, as is true of fires elsewhere, are set deliberately or accidentally by people. Although lightning can strike during the monsoon season, triggering many fires in Arizona grasslands and high-country forests, the incidence of these natural burns appears low in the Sonoran Desert. Humidity is high when lightning occurs, making it hard for a fire in the desert lowlands to get going. Before the late nineteenth century, such a fire would have been unlikely even on the days of lowest humidity, because the grasses that help keep things burning today had not yet been introduced by human immigrants to the West. The now ubiquitous European red brome unites the vegetation on hillsides that would otherwise be a mosaic of small shrubs, trees, and gravel patches. The destructive brush fires that now plague the desert during May and June feed on red brome.

Through the four years since the fire, the burnt hillside has continued to offer a very different aspect than have the unburned slopes adjacent to it. Although red brome was suppressed in the first post-fire year, the grass has come back stronger than ever in succeeding springs. Now, even in late June, when the brome cover has been long dead, the blanket of brown stalks gives the old burn an unnaturally organic look, compared with the neighboring areas of scattered shrubs set on grey gravel. The introduced tinder on the old burn waits for the next pyromaniac to light off another round in a novel cycle for which the desert is not adapted, a cycle doubly dependent on human intervention.

The Usery Mountain Mobbers

A "cold front" clipped the upper edge of Arizona yesterday, and as a result the temperature today will not break 100 degrees. There is an illusion of coolness this morning, an illusion worth treasuring since it will be 98 in a few hours.

The anonymous wash that drains a little watershed in the Usery Mountains winds through rock walls cut and shaped by flowing water from past thunderstorms. A covey of Gambel's quail scutters from under a sheltering hackberry. The birds burst into flight and disperse like buckshot into the surrounding scrub-covered plateau.

The resident great-horned owl spooks out of a mesquite anchored to the side of the wash. It parachutes silently out of view on great grey wings whose primary feathers are fringed with downy borders. The soft-edged wings let the air slip past quietly, with none of the sharp swishing sound made by the stiff-feathered wings of most birds.

Students of owl behavior have suggested that quiet flight permits owls to slip up silently on their prey, but if this is so, wouldn't all predatory birds benefit from having similar silencers on their primaries? Perhaps there are disadvantages, as well as benefits, to having the kind of wing feathers that make silent flight possible. For example, quiet wings might also be wings that are less effective in generating lift, so that great-horned owls sacrifice a component of flight efficiency for improved stealth when hunting keen-eared victims. If this hypothesis is correct, then fish-eating owls, of which there are some Asian representatives, should have stiff-edged wing feathers and noisy flight because their meals live underwater where they cannot hear approaching aerial hunters. In fact, the wings of fishing owls are endowed with stiff-edged primaries.

The wash supports neither fish nor any fish-eating owls. A rabbit pops out of a jojoba bush and scoots over the rise bordering the wash like a cartoon character shot from a cannon.

Ahead, a brown towhee and a couple of black-tailed gnatcatchers chip and chitter in a palo verde. They bounce from limb to limb as if determined to make a scene. But why are they so exercised? There seems to be nothing within the palo verde except a harmless tangle of green limbs and twigs and a complex pattern of shadows; then a flickering movement reveals two fierce yellow eyes that look out indignantly from the shade. The eyes remain disembodied for a moment before the outline of an elf owl's body forms within the visual clutter of its hiding place.

The elf owl is the smallest owl in the world, a mere fraction of the weight of its eagle-sized relative, the great-horned owl. The residual birdwatcher in me thrills more to the tiny owl than to the giant one, for they are far more rarely seen. Elf owls are actually more common than any other owl in Arizona, the great-horned owl included, but their small size and great unwillingness to flush from their daytime retreats make them invisible to most of us. But apparently not to the local songbirds, who do not take kindly either to regal great-horned owls or to fist-sized elf owls.

Harassing predators is something that prey species commonly do. Back East, every birdwatcher has seen kingbirds and crows pursuing hawks in flight, diving at them, some daredevils even landing on a raptor's back to pull out a feather or two. Owls stimulate avian mobbers around the world, too. The very birds that owls might capture and eat under the appropriate circumstances have the temerity to swoop at them, chattering and squeaking noisily, taking advantage of their victims' poor day vision.

Two black-tailed gnatcatchers mob an elf owl.

The benefit of having soft primaries (and quiet wings) if you are an owl seems fairly evident, but mobbing by songbirds has no obvious reproductive advantages for the individuals that engage in the behavior. The risks of mobbing are not subtle. To dive-bomb an owl or hawk puts a small bird within inches of powerful talons that the predator would be happy to sink into its annoyer. In our neighborhood in Tempe, screeching mockingbirds regularly pursue cats; sometimes a bird miscalculates and is nabbed by its "victim." The same thing happens occasionally in the quarrels between songbirds and hawks or owls. How can it be advantageous to spend one's valuable time and energy mobbing if this means taking a chance on being killed just to irritate a predator?

Hawks and owls that are harassed by a group of mobbing birds often appear to be annoyed, but that is about all. A kingbird cannot really harm a red-tailed hawk, and a black-throated gnatcatcher poses no physical danger even to an elf owl. Although one might suppose that prey species gain some psychological satisfaction from interrupting the daytime rest of an owl, it is hard to imagine what good this can do at the level where it really counts, that of increasing the number of offspring produced by a mobber.

A surprising number of hypotheses to account for mobbing have been invented by behavioral biologists, perhaps because mobbing is the kind of trait that begs for an explanation. When the costs of a trait advertise themselves but the benefits do not, there is a clear and appealing puzzle, one likely to attract a mob of biologists eager to compete to solve the problem.

Among the many hypotheses dreamed up by evolutionists are some familiar ones from preceding chapters, including the predator deterrence hypothesis, in which the mobbing individual informs the predator that it has been seen and that pursuit would be fruitless. Another old friend, the altruistic alarm hypothesis, states that mobbers are actually noisily alerting relatives other than offspring of the presence of a threat to their health and well-being, just as round-tailed ground squirrels sometimes sound the alarm to help a sibling or a niece stay alive. A close variant is the parental care hypothesis: self-sacrificing mobbers risk their lives in order to warn their offspring that a killer is nearby. Mobbing might also function not so much to warn the young of danger, but to distract predators from vulnerable offspring by keeping the predators looking at the mobber rather than searching for its babies.

And what about the education-of-the-young hypothesis? Parent birds might mob to direct the attention of their progeny to particular predators as part of the process of educating them about what animals are to be treated with fear and loathing. Young birds hanging back on the periphery of a mob may have their eyes opened as they safely learn details about their predators that cannot be programmed in the form of innate avoidance responses.

But then there is also the predator-move-on hypothesis, in which the mobber benefits personally by encouraging an enemy to move out of its territory and on to someone else's turf, where it will be less of a problem for the mobber and more of a problem for a nonrelative. Predators might take the advice to pack it up, since in an area noisy with screaming harassers their chance of surprising any prey, let alone the annoying mobbers themselves, has evaporated.

Nor have we exhausted the list of possibilities. Prey may mob in order to get detailed information about a particular predator, learning its identity as an individual, learning whether it is lethargic and full or alert and hungry. A mobber may use this information to decide what course of action is best in dealing with a particular predator. Should it leave the area temporarily? Can it safely ignore this particular killer?

Finally, there is an idea whose sinister Machiavellianism is positively delicious. This is the attract-the-mightier hypothesis. It appeared in a paper by Eberhard Curio, a German biologist who, with a number of colleagues, has explored mobbing behavior more thoroughly than anyone else. Curio suggests that birds mobbing a predator may attract larger, more powerful predators of another species, who may be inclined to make a meal of the lesser predator so helpfully pinpointed by the fussy little songbirds that surround it.

There are so many competing ideas on the function of mobbing that not all have been tested in even a preliminary way. Nevertheless, a considerable body of information has been developed on the subject, and all the signs point to the conclusion that the behavior serves multiple functions, with different benefits for different species in different situations, benefits that conceivably outweigh the apparent costs of the behavior.

And mobbers do things that keep the costs of mobbing under control. For example, mobbing songbirds do not take it upon themselves to commit suicide. Birds like the European great tit reserve conspicuous harassment, complete with easy-to-locate, loud mobbing calls, for *perched* enemies. When they spot a flying hawk, these songbirds are careful not to draw attention to themselves with conspicuous calls, probably because flying hawks are more likely to be hungry than perched ones and are more likely to take cheerful advantage of information about the location of prey than will a somnolent, perched predator. Unlike mobbing calls, the signals songbirds use in the presence of a flying hawk or owl are of low intensity and in a high frequency range that is harder for the predator to detect.

On the benefit side of the equation, there is support for a number of the hypotheses we have just outlined. For example, nesting gulls that mob crows distract these predators from their camouflaged eggs and cryptic nestlings, thus benefiting their young. Likewise, it is the adult barn swallow with young in a nest, not a nonbreeding adult or first-year juvenile, that is likely to mob a stuffed owl or an approaching human. Here, too, mobbing appears to be a form of parental care designed to keep predators from finding the vulnerable young of the mobbers.

Curio and his colleagues have shown experimentally that European blackbirds can be tricked into learning to mob a friarbird, an Australian species that does not occur in Europe. Some caged birds are shown an owl, which they enthusiastically mob, while others can observe the mobbers but not the owl. Instead, the onlookers see a stuffed friarbird, which they associate with the agitated mobbers. When later exposed to this object they will mob it, and other blackbirds in their company will join in the fracas. Curio's experiments show that it would be possible for an adult to educate its fledglings about what creatures it should avoid. Further, these studies make it clear that mobbing does alert and excite others, making them more wary and quicker to react to a potential predator, a result consistent with the various alarm signal hypotheses outlined earlier.

Sadly, no one has directly tested the attract-the-mightier hypothesis, and it is one that might have special relevance for birds mobbing an elf owl; the odds are excellent that any other predator lured to the resting spot of an elf owl would be bigger than the minute owl. In fact, the elf owl is so small that great-horned owls might consider it beneath their dignity to try to catch such a trivial meal.

A Norwegian behavioral biologist, Goren Högstedt, did an experiment to determine whether the loud calls of a captured prey (a starling, in this case) might not have the effect of attracting predators to the spot where the starling was in the grasp of a would-be killer. Tapes of the piercing fear screams of a manhandled starling did, indeed, draw a rogue's gallery of predators, which might under natural circumstances interfere with the hunter holding the starling before the victim had been sent to his ultimate reward. If the predators began to fight, the starling might be able to slip away, the worse for wear but pleased to be alive. Mobbing calls, however, are not the same as fear screams, and it remains to be seen whether tapes of mobbing starlings or brown towhees will bring foxes and hawks hurrying closer to see whether they might cadge a meal at the scene of the uproar.

The cost-benefit approach of behavioral ecology does not seem to be on the mind of the elf owl in the palo verde. The irritating brown towhees and black-tailed gnatcatchers have left, but I have substituted myself as a potentially even more severe threat. The owl's head jerks from right to left, and then with one more wide-eyed look the little owl pops off its perch and disappears in a flurry of silent wingbeats into a thicket of vegetation farther up the dry wash. A predator has moved on.

July

Midmorning. A faint breeze barely brushes a palo verde. The resin-covered leaves of creosote bushes are yellow and odorless.

A tiger whiptail lizard flows from one patch of shade to another. Its long tail scatters fine gravel as it slips underneath a brittlebush.

The sun suspends all other movement.

Two fledgling ravens perched on the limb of an old saguaro pant in the shadow of the massive trunk that shields them. Their fluffed black feathers create untidy outlines. Shoulder-to-shoulder, they try to outwait the heat.

One raven raises its head and carols softly to an impassive sky.

How to Win Mates
and Influence Enemies

Despite the transient dip in temperature late in the month, June was even hotter than average. The mean maximum for the month was a little over 106 degrees, and July has taken up the challenge to match or surpass that mark. On red-hot Usery Mountain this morning many saguaros are adorned with fruits that have burst open to reveal deep scarlet flesh. Near the mountaintop, a large insect buzzes noisily past at eye level. The creature cruises on unswervingly for a bit, then turns and ascends until it is in position to drop clumsily onto a fruit atop the trunk. As it lands, another individual scrambles from one fruit to another, its huge orange-knobbed antennae held up in a victory sign. The two beetles, for this is what they are, come face-to-face and grapple with their pincer jaws. The smaller competitor barely makes brief contact with the larger beetle before turning from the unequal contest to tumble away, falling into a crevice between two fruits and then scrambling out of sight of its pursuer.

The battling aeronauts are nearly two inches long, and their size, sweeping antennae, and magnificent color pattern more than compensate for their apparent lack of aerial agility. The orange elytral wing covers are attractively banded in black and covered with a thick but translucent wax that gives the insects the appearance of having been lacquered. Perhaps their most impressive features are their jaws, which protrude from their heads like the robust pincers of a pair of pliers designed for some arcane purpose. It requires no great insight to realize why this insect has the Latin name *Dendrobias mandibularis*. As is characteristic for long-horned, wood-boring beetles of the family Cerambycidae, the big-mandibled beetle also possesses antennae that are substantially longer than its body. Had the Egyptians known about this beetle, they surely would have honored it along with the sacred scarabs, which inspired so many of their artful rings and seals.

Another fight begins on the saguaro top, and one beetle is thrown or falls into space. As it drops it lifts its colorful elytra high in the air and unfolds its pliant transparent wings, which had been stored neatly under the elytral covers. With a mighty whirring the beetle struggles to gain altitude; having succeeded, it turns to sail away on a single-minded, single-direction journey. Its great antennae stream behind like windblown hairs.

A graduate student of mine, Steven Goldsmith, spent several scorching Junes and Julys watching the big-jawed beetles at a study site just off the Beeline Highway. Just off the highway means almost close enough to touch the many cars and trucks roaring along the Beeline. Tractor-trailers sent gusts of superheated wind and exhaust blasting into the desert shrubs on the shoulder of the roadway. Steve somehow became habituated to the unnerving traffic and the heat and calmly carried on, rather like the starlings that casually search for scraps of food on freeways. Necessity was the mother of habituation, in this case, because Steve had to locate a site with a large beetle population and the Beeline was the only place where he could find the numbers he needed.

The beetles transform themselves from wood-boring grubs to magnificent adults in midsummer. After emerging from the trunks of palo verdes, they search for food, which they often find in desert broom. This shrub typically grows sparsely along desert washes, but it does well at roadsides, thanks to extra water from pavement runoff. The Beeline Highway had several shoulder strips of unusually large desert brooms, each shrub growing luxuriantly to heights of two meters or more.

The big-jawed beetles and a host of other insects flock to roadside desert brooms. The plants provide rich supplies of insect food, especially of a sugary sap that oozes from little wounds in the stems of the shrub. The sap spills out into a small area that often attracts a beetle, which laps up the nutritious fluid.

Steve took advantage of the abundance of beetles drawn to broom food at the Beeline site to answer some questions about the natural history of *Dendrobias*. He was particularly interested in why only the larger males in this highly variable species possess the megajaws that give the species its Latin name. The females and the smaller males look very similar in all respects, including their modest mandibles. By measuring the lengths of the jaws of males of different sizes, Steve established that males could be placed in one of two distinct categories: the "majors" are medium to large beetles with jaws that are large in relation to their body, and the "minors" are small to medium beetles with proportionally small jaws. The two types evidently use different formulae for the development of their

A large male wood-boring beetle stands guard over a saguaro fruit that may attract mates.

jaws; majors invest relatively more in pincers than do minors, as is seen when the data are controlled for the standard effects of increasing body size on jaw development. The minors appear to use the same schedule for jaw production employed by females. Indeed, minor males must be carefully inspected to distinguish them from the other sex.

When we find an animal whose males have some distinctive structure that might be used in fighting, the rule is that it is in fact employed to this end, and *Dendrobias* is no exception to the rule. Major males are formidable fighters, thanks in part to their large jaws and in part to their large body size. They snap at, butt, and grapple with other majors on split saguaro fruits and at the ooze sites on desert broom, both of which are limited in number and valuable to males because they attract hungry females, potential mates. Large majors defeat smaller majors, forcing them to abandon an ooze; minor males do not even try to gain access to a feeding site if it is occupied by a major. As a result of the fighting advantage enjoyed by larger males, majors both occupy ooze sites far more often than do minors and account for a disproportionately large percentage of all matings.

Thus we have a species whose receptive females are concentrated at specific feeding locations, little oozing wounds on desert broom small enough to be defended by a single male. Earlier I presented the argument that male animals generally try to secure as many mates as possible because the number of females inseminated usually is closely correlated with the number of offspring a male produces. Therefore, we expect that mate-seeking males will go where they can find the greatest possible number of receptive females. If *emerging* females are receptive and males can identify likely emergence sites, males will try to defend these sites, as do empress butterflies and digger bees. If *feeding* females are sometimes receptive and males can identify especially good feeding sites, males will try to defend these sites, as do *Dendrobias* males.

Knowing the importance of mating success for males and the importance of ooze sites as a food resource for females helps explain the remarkable differences in body design between major males and females of *Dendrobias mandibularis*. There has been competition among males for control of these scarce, valuable, and defensible spots because winners have enjoyed greater than average copulatory success. The competition for mating sites has favored large males with effective fighting equipment, with the evolutionary result that some males now have the capacity to develop large bodies and larger jaws. The males that achieve the potential to be big-bodied and big-mandibled leave more descendants than do smaller individuals with more modest mandibles, thanks to the nature of the feeding ecology of females of their species.

If large males produce more surviving offspring than do small ones, why are there any minor males at all? This puzzle would be resolved if it were true that all *Dendrobias* males have the *potential* to be behemoths with massive mandibles. In order for males to achieve large size, however, they probably have to be fortunate enough to have access to plenty of high-quality food when they are larval grubs. The immature stages of *Dendrobias* feed on palo verde trunks and branches while boring through the host plant. Just as is true for digger bees, the amount of food they consume determines the size they achieve as grubs, and this in turn determines the size of the adult beetle because insects cannot grow any larger after they become adults.

Minor males probably have had bad luck as larvae. Stunted by a shortage of nutritious tissues in the palo verdes that were their homes before metamorphosis, these males fail to become big-bodied adults. Their developmental systems somehow "sense" that they are destined to be small, and so these mechanisms do not allocate the energy to produce large adult jaws, which would be ineffective weapons when wielded by a small individual. If, however, a male grub can secure relatively large amounts of nutritious wood in its palo verde, the beetle's developmental program not only yields a large adult after metamorphosis but also adopts the pathway that ultimately produces massive pincers, which *are* useful in combat if employed by a large-bodied male.

This explanation for the two types of male cerambycids is speculative, although much evidence from other insects supports the general proposition that adult body size is dependent on food consumed during the larval phase. Furthermore, many examples are known from the insects, such as digger bees, and other animals in which body size or physiological condition correlates with the competitive tactics employed by a male.

Minor males may have experienced misfortune as grubs, and they may defer to their larger rivals at ooze sites on desert broom, but they do not throw in the towel when in comes to mating. Although they assiduously avoid majors, who might well amputate their limbs in a fight, minors wander through desert broom and are quick to mount a female should they encounter one. Female *Dendrobias* will sometimes copulate with males away from a feeding site, and so minors enjoy some reproductive success. In other words, small males seem to do the best they can with the hand dealt them, as we would expect if their behavior is the product of selection for individuals that try to mate as much as possible.

The proposed relationship between localized food resources used by receptive females and the evolution of male fighting weaponry used in defending food resources can be tested. One prediction from this hypothesis is that other male cerambycids will behave like *Dendrobias* if, and only if, the females of these species become concentrated in particular places by their resource requirements. Conversely, other long-horned, wood-boring beetles whose females are not concentrated in space by the need to exploit a patchily distributed resource should have a very different mating system.

Both predictions are supported by at least some examples, although there are surprisingly few studies of cerambycids. One resource-defending species, *Monochamus scutellatus*, is a beetle whose egg-laying females prefer to oviposit in the thickest portions of fallen white pine logs. Aggressive males focus their attention on these parts of the logs, and large individuals win control of territories at these spots. Territorial males reap a reproductive reward because egg-laden females will mate with males that monopolize superior oviposition sites.

Steve Goldsmith studied another Sonoran Desert species, *Perarthrus linsleyi*, whose receptive females are widely distributed through their environment. These entirely unspectacular little cerambycids feed on the stems of brittlebush as larvae. When adults appear, they switch over to creosote bush, from whose flowers males and females extract nectar.

Happily for Steve, creosote bush is one of the commonest and most widely distributed desert plants in Arizona and is not restricted to polluted roadside verges. Therefore, he was able to conduct his study of this species on a quiet rocky hillside in west Phoenix, far from thundering trucks. On Shaw Butte, as elsewhere in the Phoenix area, creosotes are abundant, producing a plethora of small yellow flowers in late March and April. Because many creosote bushes come into flower more or less at the same time, hungry female cerambycids have a great number of plants to choose among. Therefore, there are no small feeding patches with large concentrations of receptive females, and the males of this long-horned, wood-boring beetle are not territorial; instead they fly from bush to bush, hunting for and trying to contact as many females as possible during their alloted time. A male's mating success, and thus the number of descendants he produces, appears to depend primarily on his searching ability. Males fly much more often than females as they race other males to find mates scattered through the desert.

Steve's work provides additional support for the principle that the factors that determine the distribution of females have great influence on the mating tactics of males. The lives of insects may appear chaotic and indecipherable at first glance, but Steve's considerable patience and his willingness to cope with summer on the Beeline enabled him to bring a little more order to the world of long-horned, wood-boring beetles. Not that we should rest upon Steve's laurels. Well over a thousand species of cerambycids inhabit North America and thousands more live elsewhere. Each species represents a chance to test ideas about the evolution of behavior, and it will take the work of many more dedicated graduate students before we can say that we have made good use of the diversity within even this single group of animals.

A year after Steve completed his study road crews began to widen the Beeline Highway in some stretches and to "clean up" the shoulders in others, all as part of a general plan to accommodate the increasing numbers of Phoenix residents, many of whom sensibly wish to get out of town on summer weekends and up into the mountains that can be reached by going north on the Beeline. Steve's beetle site has been graded into oblivion and the desert broom swept away in a few minutes of roadwork, erasing a miniature ecosystem populated for a few weeks each summer by one of the most magnificent creatures in the Sonoran Desert.

Bahia Laura

From Usery Peak one can see (or hear) evidence of the dominant life form of the Sonoran Desert in all sectors of the compass. People have left their mark everywhere, not just along the highways. To the south the Central Arizona Project canal, which will carry salty Colorado River water to central Arizona, forms a moat between the mountain and the city of Mesa. The corner of another water project, the western tongue of Saguaro Lake impounded behind Stewart Mountain Dam on the Salt River, is visible to the north. To the southwest the Red Mountain Development Company's immense bulldozers have scraped the beginnings of a new golf course in the desert. A patch of outrageous green and blue on the other side of Bush Highway reveals an established course centered around an arrogantly large water hazard. To the west, behind Red Mountain, the earlier development of Fountain Hills covers the bajadas near the McDowell Mountains in a network of self-consciously curved roads. The huge fountain that is the trademark of this community throws a geyser into the air. There is gunfire in the northeast from the rifle club, whose members continually pump lead into targets backed by a desert hillscape. In the east and southeast Apache Junction's trailer courts have sprawled over thousands of acres, and this rapidly growing part of Greater Phoenix has begun to shoulder its way to the very base of the Superstition Mountains.

From the peak, binoculars reveal small forms drifting from north to south on the Salt River where it flows out from beneath Stewart Mountain Dam: more people, river-runners floating on black inner tubes along a stretch of river that flows at the imperial wish of the Salt River Project, which controls the releases from Saguaro Lake. In the late spring and early summer, if winter rains have poured abundant runoff into the Salt River far upstream in the White Mountains, the Project has "excess" water that must be released or else the upstream dams will overflow and collapse, producing a disaster in downtown Phoenix that would make the national news.

At these times the Salt River flows briskly between Stewart Mountain and Granite Reef dams as it pretends once again to be a living desert river with a mind of its own. The cold water coming from the bottom of Saguaro Lake feels wonderful when it is 110 degrees in the shade.

A tidal wave of people comes to the river to go tubing on summer weekends. The United States Forest Service is responsible for that portion of the Salt River used by tubers, for it flows through the southwestern part of Tonto National Forest. The Forest Service has contracted with a concessionaire to provide bus service to points along the river. At the company's warehouse off Bush Highway, inner tubes fill the cavernous building and cars fill the parking lot.

Clutching our enormous rented tubes, my family and I leave the bus at a dusty, upstream drop-off point and hike down though a thin line of riverbank mesquites. The refrigerated river water leaves us gasping as we settle into our tubes and push out into the shallows. Caught by the even current, we drift down the middle of the river in the early morning; a great blue heron flies just overhead.

Rounding a bend, a rocky chute draws us forward. The river shoots down the chute and sweeps us out of our daydreams for a moment. Tubers before, and tubers behind. A spotted sandpiper, disturbed by drifting people, hurries across the water on stuttering wings, its cries floating away on mesquite-scented air. With only brief bursts of speedy travel created by occasional rapids, our journey is leisurely and the morning well advanced by the time we reach the Blue Point Bridge. A crowd of new arrivals piles down to the river from another bus stop, a potential departure point for us. I am inclined to call it quits, but my children, exhilarated by the morning's experience, urge that we continue.

By now we are part of a great flotilla of humans, feet and rumps submerged in water, legs, heads, and upper torsos exposed to a sun that becomes ever more brutal as the day progresses. The Lucy's warblers and verdins stop singing from the mesquites, and in their place the murmur of the crowd's voices grows, accented by rock music provided by floating radios. I apply sunscreen more and more frequently.

Many tubers tow beer-filled coolers attached to their inner tubes. Some hurl their empties at strategically located huge wire enclosures with bulls-eyes that stare at the drifting throng. Trash piles high in and around the receptacles.

The river slows to a crawl in long stretches. Fragments of white Styrofoam coolers huddle together in foamy eddies or lie helplessly trapped among the straw-colored reeds on the edge of the water. Silver glints from aluminum cans that have sunk to the river bottom. Other cans, still afloat, join us as we paddle forward, slowly turning, turning in the gentle current.

Amidst the Salt River navy of white-skinned, black-tubed drifters, I am irresistibly reminded of another aquatic experience. When I was twenty and traveling on my own along the Patagonian coast of Argentina, I heard of a place called Bahia Laura, where the sand dunes were littered with the artifacts of Tehuelche Indians. In the year when Charles Darwin visited Argentina during his voyage around the world in the *Beagle*, the Argentine caudillo General Rosas was well into his genocidal campaign against the native Patagonians, a campaign that ended only when the Tehuelches were all but exterminated. Tehuelche culture is memorialized only by the arrowheads, awls, spear points, scrapers, stone knives, potsherds and bolas that lie in forgotten encampments in sand dunes on the Patagonian coast. The Tehuelches had gathered in Bahia Laura in the past to kill sea lions, which no longer breed in the area. To get to Bahia Laura I enlisted the aid of Sr. Baines, who owned a rundown estancia of desolate saltbush plains on the far side of the estuary at Puerto Deseado. He had hired a crew of Chilean laborers to extract guano from a cormorant colony on an island in Bahia Laura sixty miles to the south, and he agreed to let me accompany two men driving down to drop off supplies for his isolated workers.

Before our departure Sr. Baines, whose English ancestry was only a faint memory in his family history, took me aside conspiratorially to warn me in Spanish about the two men who would be transporting me to Bahia Laura. The two Chileans had spent the afternoon drinking with Baines in a grey bar in dingy Puerto Deseado. I stood in the dirt street and uncertainly digested the information I had just received. My sullen companions stood nearby in full gaucho regalia, bombachas billowing in the dusty wind, broad belts covered in pesos, silver knives thrust into their belts.

In the early evening the two Chilean ranchhands and I crossed the estuary in a small boat and climbed into an ancient truck parked on the other side. It took us five hours to drive to Bahia Laura over rutted desert tracks that wound along the abandoned coast. We lurched, bumped, and ground our way through the cold night. During one brief stop I saw the outline of a distant flamingo, immobile on a salt pan that glowed under a luminous moon.

After midnight my companions let me out in the sand dunes at Bahia Laura before going the short distance remaining to the shacks occupied by Baines's employees. From the truck I unloaded two quarts of water, a sleeping bag, a tent, my camera, two bars of chocolate, three cans of Argentine spam, two packets of crackers, and three oranges. I crawled into my sleeping bag, pulled the canvas tent over me, and fell into an exhausted sleep.

I awoke just after sunrise in the middle of a great sweep of flattened sand dunes with one very small tree on the horizon. The tree crouched submissively, facing inland away from the winds sweeping onto the austere brown coast from the rich blue South Atlantic Ocean. Oystercatchers stood in squadrons among rocky tidal pools, while in the sand dunes Magellanic penguins brayed like donkeys in the cold morning. My impromptu campsite bordered a vast colony of thousands of these birds. No one had told me they were at Bahia Laura, because Patagonians take Magellanic penguins for granted or despise them as competitors for South Atlantic fish. For three days I carefully rationed my meager supply of food while watching penguins and searching for Indian relics, which were present in greater abundance and variety than I had dared dream possible when I began my trip to Bahia Laura. Scanning the litter of stones and chipped rock blanketing the dunes, my eye would fall upon a fragment with a purposeful edge, a piece that sometimes would become a superb projectile point or finely crafted stone awl when I plucked it from the sand. The Tehuelche artifacts, perfectly symmetrical, highly colored, well balanced, fully satisfied the senses of touch and vision. Their beauty and abundance said a little about the sad history of the now unpeopled coast.

During these three days I saw another human only once, when one of the Chileans brought me more drinking water, the first of several generous gifts from Baines's employees, who themselves lived under conditions of extraordinary isolation and privation.

Baines had promised vaguely to pick me up in a couple of days, but he did not come on the second or the third day, and by the afternoon of day three I had exhausted my food. Hungry and dirty, I decided that a swim might revive my spirits, which had flagged under the weight of wondering when Baines would return. And I certainly needed a wash.

The sun had reappeared after dark squalls that scuttled one after the other along the barren coast at midday. A great flock of sandpipers whirled over the tidal rocks, twisting and flashing, a single body, first brown, then white. Down in a sandy cove a large crèche of young penguins waited, standing shoulder to shoulder, white belly to black back. The mass shuffled uneasily as I approached. A few birds bolted for the water, but most stayed ashore while I undressed some distance away.

After I shed my grubby clothing, which had taken on the rich and penetrating aroma of penguin guano, I walked into the frigid but wonderfully cleansing water of the cove. Many penguins panicked and joined me in the ocean, exchanging pompous uprightness for the buoyant horizontal pose they use in the water. In the shallow embayment dozens swam and dove near me, their original fear quickly forgotten once I submerged to dogpaddle among them. Their faces were marked with black lines on white, with a small pink patch near their powerful black bills. Now and then a startled penguin would dart off, porpoising ahead in a series of wonderfully fluid leaps.

The South Atlantic was too cold for a long swim and I did not wish to be in the water should a shark come penguin-hunting. But the swim felt good and the Patagonian penguins had been pleasant swimming companions, despite the fishy smell of their bespattered nesting area.

In most respects the penguins were more intriguing than are the tubers bobbing down the Salt River with me, many of the latter well into their second six-pack. We drift for miles below the bridge. By the time we eventually reach a pick-up point far downstream, even my boys have become subdued under the now intense heat of the advanced day and the pressure of the huge crowd. My once white legs are now pink, on their way to red. An armada of tubers continues on, riding high in the regulated current, filling the air with hoots of forced delight.

Pleasant Memories

Since the area would change from a riverine to a lake-type habitat, many areas which provided pleasant memories would be lost.   — Environmental Impact Statement on Orme Dam and Reservoir, Bureau of Reclamation

A hint of moisture rides in the air. The humidity comes from the first subtropical air mass of the summer moving up from the Gulf of California. A thin line of clouds hovers above the mountains on the northern horizon, and from the south a blanket of grey inches toward Usery Mountain.

Usery Peak overlooks all the land that was to be under Orme Lake, the reservoir behind the proposed Orme Dam, which was to have been built at the confluence of the Salt and Verde rivers. Orme Lake would have flooded 25,000 acres of land, displacing an estimated 118,000 zebra-tailed lizards, and ending the tubers' entertainment forever by drowning all but a fragment of the Salt

River between Stewart Mountain Dam and the Granite Reef Diversion Dam.

But the story of Orme Lake has a happy ending; to almost everyone's surprise, Orme Dam never got off the drawing board, thanks to a fortuitous combination of Indians and cactus-huggers, as conservationists are disparagingly called by some Arizonans. First, the Audubon Society advertised the fact that a couple of pairs of bald eagles, part of a tiny southwestern population, nested along affected portions of the Salt and Verde rivers. Federal law frowns on the destruction of habitat needed for an endangered species. Bald eagles in the Southwest are few and they need running water for their fishing grounds; they show no enthusiasm at all for the big stagnant reservoirs so popular with government agencies.

The eagle problem could probably have been "solved" in a way that satisfied the proponents of Orme Dam, if not the eagles themselves, but there were other difficulties as well. The Yavapais living on the Fort McDowell Indian Reservation failed to jump at the opportunity to relinquish their claim to the land bordering the Verde River that was destined to go under when Orme Dam went up. When Orme Dam was planned, 279 Indians lived on the reservation, the descendants of a nomadic culture that had once occupied an area of more than nine million acres in central and western Arizona. Just ten years after the first Anglo intrusion into the lower Verde River (a trapping party of forty-eight that passed through in 1865), those Yavapai that had survived a decade of displacement by white settlers and warfare with the United States Army were shipped out to the San Carlos Apache Reservation, an environment far different from the one they considered home. Twenty-five years later, federal authorities recognized their right to return to a fragment of their historic lands. The U.S. Government purchased about 25,000 acres on the Verde River from the whites who had claimed the land. With the creation of a reservation for the Yavapai, the Indians returned from the San Carlos area as soon as they could and lived as best they could, although about half the tribe died during the terrible influenza epidemic of 1917–18. They were always a poor people, but when they were offered top dollar to give up 15,000 acres of their reservation to accommodate Orme Lake they turned the dambuilders down. As the Environmental Impact Statement noted, "Although the tribe would be economically compensated for the loss of land, no mitigation is possible for the feelings they attach to the land."

If the Department of the Interior had really wanted Orme Dam, the Indians, like the eagles, would probably have been firmly educated about the need for progress and the importance of the greater good. They were, after all, a tribe of a few hundred whose wishes had to be balanced against what was desirable for hundreds of thousands of downstream Phoenicians, or so the advocates of the dam stated noisily and often. But Orme Dam had another fundamental defect. It was going to be expensive, with an initial estimate of six hundred million dollars in construction costs, an estimate that cynics (or realists) felt would prove to be on the low side when the final bill was presented. At a time of increasing federal deficits and growing reluctance among eastern legislators to fund western water projects, Orme Dam was an expendable, pricey item.

Out to the Yavapais, therefore, came James Watt, then Secretary of the Interior, to announce that he was on the side of the Indians, the eagles, and the angels, in this instance, and that Orme Dam was dead. Watt had few other opportunities to make similar announcements, and he made the most of this one.

The demise of Orme Dam saved many miles of the Salt and Verde rivers, and a good many acres of old floodplain and desert flats with a healthy population of creosote bush. People would get excited about bald eagles even if they were not endangered in the Southwest, and rightly so, for they are wonderfully impressive as they glide above a river, white head and white tail radiant in Arizona sunshine. Creosote bush, on the other hand, stimulates considerably less excitement. It is a very common plant in the Sonoran Desert, and few have rhapsodized about its appearance; it is fair to say that it is a spindly shrub (rarely more than six feet tall) with a handful of sticky little yellow-green leaves. Creosote bush occasionally puts out a bouquet of diminutive yellow flowers, but even then it cannot be promoted as a tourist attraction.

Despite the fact that it is neither rare nor impressive in appearance nor a symbol at any level of government, creosote bush is well worth having around. The undrowned populations of the plant growing on the bed of nonexistent Orme Lake offer some special attractions that are absent in artificial desert lakes. For one thing, the plant is the only home of *Ligurotettix coquilletti*, a small brown grasshopper that feeds almost exclusively on creosote bush.

At midday in mid-July, when almost everything else has shut up, gone underground, left for the mountains, or headed for the coast, creosote grasshoppers are out and about, clicking a little defiant midsummer's song. Here is concrete acoustical evidence that something is still alive in the desert, something that can thumb its nose (so to speak) at the oppressive heat and fierce dryness. Admittedly, trying to track a song to its singer is a frustrating job, because the tick-tick of the insect is either ventriloquistic or the grasshoppers are superbly adept at spotting approaching people and slipping behind a creosote limb, where they crouch out of sight.

Of course the grasshoppers are not singing their tuneless song for anyone's entertainment, but instead are engaged in an intensely competitive enterprise that is all about sex. To investigate the sex lives of *Ligurotettix coquelletti*, several teams of biologists have ignored summer heat and overcome the difficulties of locating the grasshoppers in their creosote bush hideouts. These biologists have established that male creosote grasshoppers are territorial, usually with only one chirping male per creosote bush. When Daniel Otte and Anthony Joern captured, marked, and released singing males in a plot of creosote bush desert they found that the singers tended to stay put, sometimes residing in a particular creosote shrub for weeks on end.

More recent studies by Michael Greenfield and Todd Shelly have revealed additional details about the grasshopper's territorial system. Like Otte and Joern, they studied the insect by marking populations of males in plots of creosote bush flats. When Greenfield began his study he sought Otte's advice on how to capture his subjects and was told to grasp them firmly but gently between thumb and forefinger. Attempts to put this advice into practice soon reduced Greenfield to despair, because the males in his study plot were not only hard to locate but reluctant to let him get thumb and forefinger anywhere near their bodies. Greenfield now uses two clear plastic cups of different sizes, which he eases into position about a grasshopper before jamming the cups together with the prey inside.

Greenfield and Shelly discovered early on that there were exceptions to the rule of one bush, one grasshopper. They marked a large population of males, therefore, in order to find out why several hoppers aggregated in some bushes while leaving others completely unoccupied, even though these shunned shrubs were not obviously

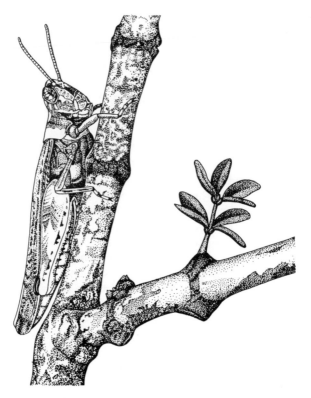

A creosote bush grasshopper aboard a creosote stem.

different in size or density of foliage. They found that when several males "share" a creosote bush, one male tends to be dominant. This male sings lustily, while the others call sporadically or not at all. When the dominant male hears or spots a moving rival in his bush, he jumps through the shrub and approaches his opponent, waving his hindlegs about in a threatening display. This intimidating action almost always suffices to send the other male bounding off in retreat, but if the co-occupant stands his ground the two males may wrestle briefly on the stem before the subordinate concedes defeat and withdraws.

Even so, losers may hang out in an occupied creosote bush, calling when they can, but otherwise staying as inconspicuous as possible so as not to draw the violent attention of the dominant male. However, if the territorial resident is removed, a previously subordinate male in the bush will soon begin to sing steadily, adding his ticks to those coming from neighboring creosotes occupied by resident males. Therefore, the quiet lurkers are not congenitally incapable of singing but instead defer to a territorial rival.

If a male remains largely quiet he cannot be easily detected and driven away by his territorial bushmate, but he also cannot advertise his presence to females. Because receptive females are attracted to singing males, there would seem to be no point to a male remaining in a creosote bush unless he were to sing. Shouldn't silent males pack up and head for a new bush where they could safely tick out their sexual song? Indeed, a male that is completely silent in a bush with a dominant rival often does spend part of the day in an otherwise unoccupied shrub where he sings steadily, only to shut up again when he moves back into the territory of his social superior. So why don't such males stay where they can safely sing unharassed by another male?

One possibility is that silent males may be acoustically inactive while remaining sexually lively. In fact, creosote grasshoppers provide yet another example of an insect species whose males can practice more than one mate-acquiring tactic. A lurking "satellite" male sometimes spots a female coming into his bush before the singing male detects her; if he does, the silent male may intercept her and mate. The territorial male continues signaling, unaware that he has lost a copulation to a co-resident male that he has socially dominated but has not been able to force out of his creosote bush. Therefore, a silent male can sometimes succeed in reproducing, even though he does not have his own bush to use as a territorial soapbox from which to broadcast a song of attraction to females.

All the evidence indicates, however, that although satellite males may mate surreptitiously, their successes are few and far between. Singing territory owners copulate much more frequently than do the subordinates in their bushes. For one thing, in order to mate, a subordinate must court a female first, and this requires leg-waving displays (very similar in form to the threat displays that males use to put down a rival). Keen-eyed residents can spot these movements at a considerable distance and are quick to intervene, disrupting most courtships before the subordinate can induce the female to mate.

Therefore, even though subordinates reproduce occasionally they cannot hope to match the sexual prowess of the territorial males with whom they coexist. We still have to figure out why they do not leave bushes occupied by territorial despots for unoccupied creosotes. Because there were no consistent differences between the occupied and avoided bushes in size or other obvious properties, Greenfield and Shelly wondered if there might not be something subtly wrong with the chemistry of avoided bushes. They guessed that there might be variation in creosote leaves that affected their nutritional value to the grasshoppers, with females avoiding poor-quality bushes. If this were so, males would have nothing to gain sexually by defending bushes of low nutritional value.

With the aid of a biochemist they set about analyzing the compounds present in bushes that were popular with males (year after year) and those that were consistently shunned. Creosote bush gets its name from the tarry smell of its resin-covered leaves, and the waxy layer covering creosote leaves contains large amounts of nordihydroguariaretic acid (NDGA), a formidable-sounding substance that prevents oxidation of materials and so may interfere with metabolic cycles within grasshoppers and other herbivores. Chemical analysis revealed that the bushes popular with creosote grasshoppers produced waxy leaf covers relatively low in NDGA. Furthermore, when Greenfield and company offered foliage high in NDGA to laboratory-bound grasshoppers they ate less than when they were given creosote foliage low in this key material. Finally, a higher proportion of males confined to cheesecloth enclosures on low-quality bushes died than did males similarly caged on bushes that past records had shown were favored by the hoppers.

The battery of tests suggests that males (and females) like certain creosote bushes because they provide less toxic food than do other bushes. Males that can defend these superior sites attract females that will stay put, feeding on the food in the territory and mating with the owners of the shrubs, just like the females of big-jawed cerambycids in desert broom. Males that cannot monopolize a high-quality bush are between a rock and a hard place. They can move to a low-quality creosote, but the leaves there will not satisfy females and keep them around to be courted and mated. Furthermore, to the extent that the male feeds on his own territory he may be poisoning himself and reducing the number of days he has to spend calling for mates in a creosote flat. The alternative is to move into a high-quality bush with a dominant rival, there to feed on nutritious leaves, at least, but to lead a very low-profile sex life. The fact that many males shift back and forth between active solo signaling in a poor bush and more or less silent co-residence in a good bush hints that the two alternatives may yield about equal reproductive chances. The loser males are probably doing the best they can, but something prevents them from becoming what all male creosote grasshoppers aspire (unconsciously) to become — the alpha male in a creosote bush with tasty, nutritious, nontoxic foliage that will feed a large number of receptive females.

I doubt that even one of the advocates of Orme Dam was aware of the summer soap operas playing out in the creosote bushes that would have been drowned under Orme Lake. Entomologists that do know what is going on might claim that the rich drama of grasshopper life supported by creosote bush is evidence enough of the value of the plant. Further, they might argue that equally instructive stories will emerge when biologists get around to documenting the social behavior of other creosote bush specialists, which include species of walking sticks, geometrid moths, certain katydids, weevils, and buprestid beetles, each of which probably has a reproductive strategy intertwined with elements of the host plant's biology. Botanists can pontificate with equal fervor that we do not have to justify creosote bush in entomological terms, because its own adaptations for living and reproducing in a severe environment are fascinating enough to warrant admiration and respect for this common and unassuming species. They are both right, and so we have two more reasons for joining the Yavapai in applauding the demise of Orme Dam.

July's Saguaro

By mid-July the saguaros have lost all their flowers and most of their fruits, the empty husks of which have fallen to the ground where they lie seedless. Some of the capsules have split into star-shaped forms whose inner surface still retains the brilliant red coloring of their tissues. These remnants look like crimson flowers on the gravel beneath the cacti, which stand austerely over the detritus of their reproductive season, undecorated arms raised in permanent triumph. Or surrender?

The many animals that once sipped saguaro nectar or ate red saguaro fruits or black saguaro seeds must find some new resource in the desert or go elsewhere. What sustains those that stay behind? The litter of fallen saguaro fruits has been worked over by woodrats and then dried by the sun to the consistency of charcoal briquets.

From the inorganic soil near a really big saguaro, the hairy brown legs of a tarantula poke out of the giant spider's burrow. The time of year approaches when year-old male tarantulas go walking across the desert in search of the homes of females, who may be twenty years their seniors.

The massive saguaro is dozens of years old, perhaps even more than two hundred years old. It has survived winter freezes, summer windstorms, bacterial attacks, a volley of bullets. One of its seven arms droops down and up again in a great loop, the result of a cold spell in which the tissue connecting the arm to the trunk froze long enough to cause the arm to wilt but not to die. In the years since that cold day the arm has circled back up to present its growing surface to the sun again. The elegant arm looks like a patriarchal mammoth's tusk, a relict of the Pleistocene, when mammoths and giant ground sloths occupied these desert lands.

The empty husks of saguaro fruit litter the desert gravel in July.

Cooperative Killers and Lovers

AHarris's hawk flops off its saguaro-top perch and pounds away on heavy wingbeats before gaining a little altitude. It then banks in a gentle arc, gliding now, exposing its rufous shoulders and white tail band, which are nicely set off by the blue-grey to black plumage that covers most of the rest of its body. The beautiful bird utters a scratchy, herniated call as it turns in the sky.

I see Harris's hawks on most of my desert walks. Although they do not appear to enjoy my company, fleeing as soon as they spot me, they are an unusually social animal. In fact, Harris's hawk is a member of an exclusive club of birds that engages in polyandry, communal breeding, and year-round sociality. Pairs of this unusual bird are sometimes assisted by one or two other adults, so that trios and quartets live together during the nesting season. After breeding, the young of the year often remain with those that reared them, creating a society of up to seven hawks, although the average is between four and five.

In almost all other hawks a breeding pair cares for its offspring without assistance from any auxiliary adults, and once fledged the young birds disperse fairly quickly from the parental territory. Harris's hawk, therefore, is an exceptional case, and exceptions invite an accounting.

Why should some adults join others in a breeding attempt instead of finding a partner and establishing their own nesting territories? As it turns out, there apparently are two different kinds of breeding groups among Harris's hawks. First, on some nesting territories a female is assisted by two fully adult males, both of which may copulate with her preceding and during the egg-laying phase. This practice constitutes polyandry, with the single female having two "mates," although in most *menages a trois* one male apparently dominates the other, and the alpha male has greater sexual access to the female than does the subordinate. It is likely, therefore, that the alpha male fathers most or even all of the offspring produced by the female, if we assume that a higher frequency of copulation translates into a higher probability of fertilizing a female's eggs.

Other units are not so sexually complex, consisting as they do of a single breeding pair of adults and a number of young birds, none of which mates with the female. These groups of reproducing adults and helping, nonreproducing auxiliaries are said to engage in communal breeding.

The critical point is that there are two kinds of assistants: those that mate with the female (although to a lesser degree than does her primary partner), and those that forgo reproduction altogether and instead devote themselves solely to the care of the breeding pair and the resulting young. In both cases, the big question is how such self-sacrificing behavior can evolve if natural selection acts on the basis of differences in reproductive success, favoring individuals that reproduce maximally. The question has intrigued enough evolutionary biologists to produce the suggestion that some Harris's hawks give up or reduce their chances of reproducing by becoming assistants because their chances of reproducing on their own happen to be next to nothing. The idea here is much the same as that employed in the making-the-best-of-a-bad-job arguments presented earlier in discussions of the low-payoff tactics used by small male digger bees and nonterritorial creosote grasshoppers. If a particular Harris's hawk has little chance of breeding successfully as one of a monogamous pair, it does not have a great deal to lose by becoming an auxiliary. A subordinate male in a polyandrous trio may be sacrificing very little by helping the alpha male and the female in return for a slight chance of fertilizing an egg. In some populations of the hawk, adult males greatly outnumber adult females for unknown reasons, so that there is no way that every adult male can acquire his very own partner. Males unable to induce a female to form an exclusive bond may salvage some reproductive opportunity by joining a pair as a helpful subordinate, thereby gaining a small but measurable chance to father one or more chicks produced by the female. Even if the subordinate fails to reproduce while it is a helper, it might have a chance to become the female's primary partner should the alpha male die while the trio is together.

Although the secondary male in a polyandrous arrangement has some chance of producing a descendant that breeding season, the same cannot be said of the nonbreeding youngsters that sometimes help pairs. Males in this category might also be attempting (presumably without conscious awareness of their ultimate goal) to ingratiate themselves with a potential future mate. But this need not be the main result of their actions in order for helping behavior to be evolutionarily advantageous to one-year-old males, if they help selectively. Young males probably have little chance of defeating older, more experienced rivals in the competition for scarce females. In these circumstances yearlings may leave more copies of their genes by helping their parents produce additional siblings. As we noted in the case of alarm calls and ground squirrels, when relatives help each other they promote the welfare of their shared genetic heritage, and in so doing they may compensate for some decrease in their personal reproductive output.

Young helpers invariably are the offspring of the pair they assist. If their help results in the production of additional brothers and sisters that would not have existed without their extra aid, then the additional siblings represent a genetic contribution by the helpers. This contribution can be added to the lifetime genetic account that measures their total effect on the survival and propagation of their genes.

The evidence concerning the impact of helpers on parental productivity is not overabundant for Harris's hawks, but existing data indicate that trios generate somewhat more fledglings per breeding attempt than do pairs, and that pairs with helpers probably have more breeding attempts per year than do pairs working on their own. The reason helpers might have a beneficial effect on the reproductive success of the birds they help leads us back to the difficulties of making a living in the Sonoran Desert.

Harris's hawks specialize in the capture of speedy cottontails and black-tailed jackrabbits, and these are not the easiest of animals to subdue. In the first place, desert cottontails sensibly do little except hide in the shade during the middles of most desert days. For much of the year a hawk has only a few hours each dawn and dusk to find a rabbit. Cottontails and jackrabbits also are fairly large, relative to the hawk, with big jackrabbits weighing about three times as much as their would-be killers. All of this suggests that solo hunters often may not make a kill for several days running; the failure to feed over this period could damage the adult hawk's survival chances, as well as those of hungry nestlings or fledglings dependent on it.

To reduce the odds of going without food for several consecutive days, Harris's hawks hunt cooperatively. James Bednarz studied the birds in New Mexico. He showed that from two to six hawks leapfrog through their foraging territory together, always keeping in visual contact and ready to come together should a rabbit be spotted by any one hunter. If the prey tries to hide under a bush, one or

A trio of Harris's hawks cooperates in a jackrabbit hunt.

two in the party descend into the shrub to flush the unfortunate prey back into the open, where the other hawks are poised to pounce. As the rabbit flees from one enemy, it may unwittingly head for an unpleasant surprise prepared by another member of the band.

When a hunting team makes a collective kill there is plenty of food to go around and the birds are good about sharing it. If we assume that a party of five hawks kills just two rabbits every three days, all the birds will get most of the calories they need to stay alive. Bednarz found that the hawks he watched made the requisite number of captures. Thus, a combination of factors, including (1) an unbalanced sex ratio, (2) the large size, elusiveness, and limited availability of rabbit prey, and (3) the possibility of helping relatives, has contributed to the evolution of cooperative hunting and communal breeding in this species of hawk. Individuals of other raptors in which adult females are as numerous as adult males, or that hunt smaller, more manageable prey, have less to gain by banding together, either to rear their young or to forage for victims. The red-tailed hawk, one of the commonest hawks in the Sonoran Desert, is a strict individualist, hunting alone and breeding in the traditional fashion, one pair without auxiliaries.

The point is that there is nothing inherently superior about families that stay together. Cooperation only works for Harris's hawks because social individuals enjoy higher reproductive success than do solitary members of their species. This result arises because of the peculiar set of environmental pressures acting on Harris's hawks. Red-tails deal with different circumstances and problems; given their sex ratio and the kinds of prey they hunt, social red-tails probably would actually suffer reduced reproductive success.

To understand the diversity of animal behavior it is probably best to be a relativist, and so able to see that what promotes individual reproductive success in one setting might well be a handicap in another environment. Many people believe that humans are an exemplar for all living things, offering an absolute goal of advanced sociality toward which all birds and mammals, insects and arachnids are slowly moving. According to this self-centered view, Harris's hawks are a little bit farther up the social ladder than are red-tails. But red-tailed hawks can hold their heads up, if it is correct that a solitary lifestyle is the superior mode for dealing with the special problems they face.

Of Leks and Carpenter Bees

Grey skies and grey haze surround the Superstitions and the Usery Mountains. The pre-monsoon atmosphere is palpable; but where is the relief of a thunderstorm? There have been encouraging buildups of cumulus clouds in the afternoons and one evening a dust storm rolled through town, but the rains have yet to come.

On the top of Usery Mountain a little after 6:00 A.M. the air carries a distinctive scent, sweet and sharply perfumed. The odor trail leads to a big orange bee hovering noisily in the center of a creosote bush. This is a carpenter bee, *Xylocopa varipuncta*, whose males hover by bushes in the late afternoon on the mountain in March, April and May. At the start of the summer only a handful of afternoon males remained, suggesting that the flight season of the bee would end soon, perhaps sometime in June. But a few individuals have stayed the course, shifting their activity to the very early morning, probably to avoid the unbearable afternoon temperatures of full summer.

The Sonoran Desert's *Xylocopa varipuncta* is just one of 125 species of carpenter bees in the Western Hemisphere alone. Thanks to their large size, striking color, and conspicuous behavior, we know something about male behavior of species found in South Africa, Kenya, Israel, the Galapagos Islands, Costa Rica, Mexico, Brazil, Australia, and the United States. Not that there is a surfeit of information on the behavior of *Xylocopa* bees; only a handful have been observed in any detail. Large gaps exist in our knowledge of the lives and lifestyles of even the better-studied species, a category to which *Xylocopa varipuncta* belongs.

Carpenter bees around the world are noted for the ability of females to cut elaborate nesting burrows in wood. In the Southwest, females of *Xylocopa varipuncta* construct their nests in cottonwood limbs or chunks of firewood in suburban backyards. They collect masses of pollen and nectar for the production of a brood ball, a sphere of food they place in an arm of their nests. After laying an egg on the brood ball, the female constructs a thin "particle-board" partition that seals off one cell and forms the back wall of a new one, which receives a new brood ball and egg. The cell partition consists of chips of wood gnawed from within the nest tunnel and glued together with a salivary secretion. Within their private chambers eggs hatch into grubs, and grubs feast on the brood ball, polishing it off in about two weeks. The larval carpenter bees become pupae and pupae metamorphose into adults. A female may be able to collect enough food to produce eight or so offspring in one season. Even after becoming adults these offspring usually will remain with her in the nest, especially the males, which are dependent upon their mothers and sisters for regurgitated nectar meals. Adult males almost never forage for themselves. During the spring phase of the breeding season males leave their natal nests for just an hour or two in the late afternoon. Carrying a supply of donated nectar in their crops, which occupy a large portion of the abdomen, they fly to certain shrubs on ridgetops and peaks or to prominent trees in dry washes. There they hover and hover, waiting for a receptive female to arrive.

Males possess a massive paired gland in the thorax, which contains a volatile blend of trans-geranylgeraniol, trans-farnesal, and 3,7,11-trimethyl-2,7,10-dodecatrienal, an intimidating cocktail of compounds to pronounce but one with a pleasant scent. It seems likely that this blend constitutes the sex pheromone of the species, designed to attract females to a "calling" male. While hovering, males release the substance and use their legs to rub the fluid over their bodies, the better to disperse the scent downwind. The sweet perfume is so intense that it is easy for a human to detect and doubtless more evident still to passing female carpenter bees.

Not that females are particularly common visitors to hovering males. In about fifty hours of watching males at ridgetop creosote bushes, an Australian biologist, Andrew P. Smith, and I saw fewer than two females per hour approach a bush where a male waited. Because females are jet black, not orange, recognizing a female visitor poses no problem for either a human observer or a waiting male bee, who is generally quick to react.

And an odd reaction it is. Rather than fly toward a female buzzing slowly about his station, the male flies to and lands upon a little sprig of creosote or ironwood leaves; grasping them with his legs, he clambers up an inch or two, appearing to rub his legs and the underside of his body on the vegetation, apparently scent-marking the leaves. He usually repeats this maneuver energetically several times, dropping from his landing site after each bout of rubbing to hover and look about.

A male carpenter bee hovers at his lek display site in a creosote bush.

In order to determine whether color cues are the signal that triggers the male's land-and-rub display, I painted some bee-sized wooden cylinders black and others orange. With these models tied by pale threads to a six-foot classroom pointer I marched into South Mountain Park to conduct an experiment. I dangled first one, then the other wooden model near a hovering male. The orange fake male was inspected by hovering carpenter bees and was sometimes even buzzed by an irate individual, but only the black fake females stimulated males to scramble onto their landing sites. Thus, males can discriminate between visiting females and males on the basis of color cues alone.

But what is the effect of the male's actions on the real thing? For the most part, females give no hint that they are impressed with the male's display. The vast majority of visiting females leave without so much as touching the displaying male, let alone mating. A mating occasionally occurs, however, always after the male has performed his routine, the female then landing on the spot the male has rubbed. The male waits until the female grips the vegetation firmly before he lands on her back for a mating that lasts about fifteen seconds and ends when the female drops from the perch. The pair separates, the male resumes hovering in his tree or shrub, and the female races off.

What a wonderfully strange business this is. If we have interpreted things correctly, males are fed by their female relatives to enable them to hover at plants on ridgelines or in washes. Potentially receptive females fly along ridges and washes searching for males, which they probably locate in part by the floral pheromone the males release. A close visit by a female triggers a paroxysm of display, in which the male presumably marks a landing site for a female. If she accepts his perfumed invitation, mating occurs. Females probably mate just once, and only after having inspected a number of males. My coworkers and I have seen several males hovering in the same bush on some afternoons, and on some occasions we have seen a female elicit display from several males before either leaving or, in a few cases, selecting one of the co-occupants at a hovering site. The other males make no move to interfere with the lucky winner.

There are many other things I wish I knew about *X. varipuncta*. Do females visit the same locations over a number of days before finally selecting a mate? Do some males return to the same hovering station on more than one day? Is a female's choice of a partner influenced by the quantity of scent he releases? Or does the ratio of component parts of the pheromone affect a male's mating chances? Or perhaps females prefer males whose distinctive chemical "signature" they recognize from previous inspection visits to hovering stations, possibly because such males are advertising their capacity to return day after day to defend a territory?

These questions arise because it appears that females *are* being choosy about the male they will mate with. In many species of insects, including the empress butterfly and cactus fly, males wait by a resource of value to females, such as a rich patch of flowers or an egg-laying site. Naturally, some females come to these spots; they may mate with the males there for a variety of reasons, not the least of which is that the male may prevent them from using the resource unless they copulate. But the shrubs and trees that hovering males of *X. varipuncta* select usually have nothing a female can use. The plants often are not in flower and so cannot attract foraging females. Even when a creosote bush used as a hovering station is flowering, there are abundant alternative sources of creosote nectar and pollen nearby that are not being guarded by males. Furthermore, the plants selected by waiting males often have no limbs large enough to accommodate the nest of a female. All of this suggests that females visit males strictly to pick a mate and for no other reason. Males hover, release their sex pheromone, and fight sedately with one another in looping chase flights that usually (but not always) result in the departure of one male and the resumption of hovering by the "winner," who may very occasionally get a chance to display to a visiting female.

This kind of mating system has evolved in any number of other animals, including some famous birds and mammals. For example, male sage grouse gather in groups on the prairie, with each male defending a small patch of ground on which he performs his displays. Male sage grouse produce booming vocalizations, inflate their neck pouches, elevate their remarkable tail feathers, and perform foot-stamping dances, displays that even entomologists concede are more extraordinary than those of hovering carpenter bees. Female sage grouse observe and choose. After mating, females leave their partners and go off to nest on their own.

Male sage grouse and some male carpenter bees behave similarly, in that they do not defend sites that have something females need. Instead, their behavior seems designed solely to persuade females to accept their sperm and to repel other males from the display site.

Although the popular perception may be that science has nailed down most of the answers, there is still an abundance of unanswered questions about animals. For example, there is no universally accepted explanation for the evolution of leks, as the aggregations of territorial carpenter bees and sage grouse are called. Behavioral biologists have struggled to explain how such a mating system might have evolved. Intuitively, the behavior of male *Dendrobias* beetles or male digger bees seems far more sensible than that of lekking carpenter bees. The long-horned, wood-boring beetles defend resources that naturally attract females; digger bees locate emerging virgin females directly; my carpenter bees set up little empty territories on a barren peak without a female in sight.

One tentative hypothesis — let's call it the last resort hypothesis — for leks is that they evolve when the resources used by females are not distributed in patches that concentrate females at certain locations. If females are not "naturally" clustered at feeding or nesting sites, males have no "logical" places to go to search for mates. Leks form as a matter of last resort, with males forced to aggregate to display their competitive ability to discriminating females intent (unconsciously) on picking a male who may produce competitively skillful sons. The more elaborate the display the better able the male is to advertise his abilities to watching females, so the argument goes. If female carpenter bees could determine that a particular male could hover longer on a given afternoon than his rivals, or that he had shown up at a station on more days than most males, then they could conceivably choose a male whose genes would be good for their offspring. The male would have demonstrated that he possessed superb physiology for flying or that his sisters and mother were super foragers able to collect so much food that he had an abundance of fuel for his afternoon flights.

From the males' perspective, the essence of the last resort hypothesis is that they would go to other places to compete for mates if they could, but they can't, thanks to the even distribution of resources that females need. In the case of my carpenter bee, females gather pollen and nectar at an extremely wide range of flowering plants, including one of the most abundant and evenly distributed Sonoran Desert shrubs of all, the creosote bush. Thus the nature of the food used by females prevents its economic defense by males wishing to contact mates.

The last resort hypothesis is only one possible explanation. A variant of this hypothesis states that, yes, resource distribution may be even, but other factors do concentrate females traveling to and from these resources. What males are doing, according to proponents of this argument, is stationing themselves at hot spots, those places that naturally funnel females moving about in their environment. According to this hypothesis, the distribution of leks is not random but is designed instead to take advantage of "natural" concentrations of females that occur not at clumps of resources but elsewhere.

The finding that males gather on ridgelines and in washes, both of which are natural corridors or orientation guides for flying female bees, is consistent with the hot spot hypothesis. However, many more questions need answers before we can say with confidence that we really understand what male carpenter bees are doing when we find them hovering on a May afternoon or a July morning by a creosote bush on the top of a mountain in the Sonoran Desert. On Usery Peak the male I watch has been turning and circling his creosote station for more than half an hour this morning. He appears as alert now as he was earlier. An individual of another species of bee with a black abdomen and tan thorax zooms into the creosote bush, looking for even one surviving flower from which to extract a little nectar. The male carpenter bee reacts at once to the arrival of the newcomer, dashing over to the tip of a creosote limb, where he lands and rubs his body vigorously over the sparse vegetation. The visiting bee ignores the display and moves from one branch to another. But there are no flowers, only a sampler of furry white capsules that contain creosote seeds. The black-and-tan visitor sails out of the creosote and disappears, leaving the carpenter bee to hover alone as the sun rises higher in the sky.

All Used Up

A coyote yips sharply in a scrub-filled gully, but it remains hidden and slips off unseen. A solitary white-winged dove tumbles off a leafless ocotillo and clatters away. The seed cases of the ocotillo have turned dark tan and are open; they long ago spilled their seeds onto the ground where any survivors still wait for the first rain of the monsoon.

A lesser nighthawk flutters up from the ground and perches nervously on the tip of an ocotillo stalk. It leaves two grey mottled eggs resting on the bare soil, not even partly shaded by a nearby bursage. Somehow the nighthawk is able to incubate eggs while seated directly on the desert floor under the cruel sun of late July. Are the two eggs replacements for an earlier set consumed by a coyote or a curve-billed thrasher? Or are they the second clutch for a female that nested successfully in the late spring?

A reddish stone lies on the surface of a sandy wash. It is a thin, fractured stone, smaller than a hand; one edge has been chipped repeatedly. The stone is an Indian implement, a scraper or knife for cleaning hides or cutting game. Many similar stone tools rest in the sand dunes of Bahia Laura in Argentina among the nests of Magellanic penguins. Stone technologies around the world have converged on particular patterns, no doubt those that suited significant tasks especially well and that could be constructed reliably, given the fracture patterns of flint, chert, jasper, and quartz. A Tehuelche scraper from Argentina is, to my untrained eye at least, all but identical to one made by the Hohokam or Anasazi of Arizona thousands of miles away.

The Hohokam occupied central Arizona for roughly seventeen hundred years, over four times as long as European settlement in North America has lasted. But Hohokam culture ended around 1450, prior to contact with Europeans. Some believe that the modern Pima-Papagos, or Tohono O'odham, are the descendants of these ancient people, but others disagree, arguing that the Hohokam really did disappear. They left behind the remains of their adobe and semisubterranean households and the durable debris of their lives, stone flakes and tools and, especially, fragments of pottery. Many places near Usery Peak once were occupied by the Hohokam, judging by the potsherds that lie exposed on the surface after a rain, embedded in the clay that the Indians once farmed.

Most people find the decline and disappearance of the Hohokam a compelling mystery. Some archaeologists have suggested that climatic changes produced a long drought that undercut the agricultural base of the culture. Others believe these peoples were derived from and dependent upon Mesoamerican cultures to the south, and that upheavals in Mexico broke trade routes and led finally to the impoverishment and extinction of the Hohokam. Still others point to Piman myths that point to a period of political instability and wars among Hohokam villages.

I like the hypothesis that their irrigation practices, although successful for centuries, eventually led to the salinization of the soil and contributed to the collapse of Hohokam agriculture. The Indians had an extensive system of hand-dug irrigation canals, some of which passed through the neighborhood where I live, as revealed by aerial photographs taken of Tempe when it still had a fair number of cotton and alfalfa fields, all of which have now been covered by houses. The old canals, even though they had been filled, blanketed with blown soil, and tilled for years, still appeared as faint dark lines in the photographs. And there were lots of them.

Some Hohokam canals were big enough to take your breath away, over thirty feet wide and ten feet deep; others were less elaborate. The Hohokam gradually built hundreds of miles of canals to siphon water from the Gila and Salt rivers onto their gardens of squash, tepary beans, corn, and cotton. These irrigation systems were large and complex, with up to nine different villages serviced by the same network. Furthermore, at the peak of Hohokam development, there may have been well over fifty substantial villages and many lesser ones scattered up and down the Salt and Gila rivers, housing perhaps sixty thousand people. The irrigation demands of all these people probably exceeded the water available in the rivers during June and July, especially during drought years. All of this suggests that the Hohokam must have had a sophisticated political apparatus to adjudicate the water claims of different groups. You can be sure that downstream villages were not eager to have their irrigation channels go dry while people living upstream diverted all available river water to their use.

The rivers of the Southwest challenge irrigators, not only because flows change dramatically from season to season, running nearly dry before the monsoon only to flood after a series of rains, but also because the water they carry is often high in dissolved inorganic salts. These substances are carried onto fields by irrigation water and deposited there, where they build up in the soil, eventually ruining the earth for agriculture. For a time, deep watering helps flush the salts down below the root line, but eventually the salt concentrations become high enough to reduce productivity substantially no matter what remedy one applies.

I know this at first hand because I have a postage stamp garden in my frontyard (and another in the backyard) where I grow Swiss chard, broccoli, lettuce, and spinach in the winter. These plants all cope reasonably well with salty soil, but shallow waterings and additions of homemade mulch (soaked repeatedly to encourage its breakdown in my compost heap) led in the space of a few years (not a span of centuries) to such high salt levels that salt-sensitive plants like beans and squash became intolerant of my efforts at horticulture, and even the tougher species were suffering.

I had a solution in mind that was not available to the Hohokam.

I proposed to remove my salt-laden soil and replace it with one of the commercial concoctions of compost, topsoil, and sand sold as Queen Blend or Garden Special. With visions of excessively luxuriant plants — the equal of those starring in Burpee catalogs — once again growing in my garden, I carefully dug out the old soil and at considerable expense brought in ten cubic yards of new soil, a good deal more than I really needed.

My horticultural dreams were unfulfilled. Eventually I realized that something was drastically wrong with my purchase, which may have been high in price but was low in whatever it took to grow even Swiss chard. I took a sample of the stuff I had purchased to a soil analysis laboratory, where I was told that it had substantial salt concentrations but almost no nitrogen and phosphorus, a combination that explained why my garden was such a dismal failure.

If it has been depressing for me to try to deal with the degeneration of the soil I use for recreational gardening, it must have been terrifying for the Hohokam farmers to fail to solve a similar problem in their fields, one of which may very well have been beneath the same plot of land that I now use. All of this assumes that it really was an insidious, slow farming disaster that drove the Hohokam off the land their ancestors had occupied for much longer than the current United States of America has existed.

In any event, almost as impressive as the sudden collapse of the Hohokam is the extent to which they had colonized Arizona before their eventual disappearance. As I have indicated, they were everywhere. Their canals ran through Tempe, Mesa, and Phoenix. Their potsherds litter the ground in places where digger bees emerge by the Salt River well to the east of Phoenix. Whenever a developer starts digging anywhere in the metropolitan area he has a good chance of uncovering a settlement site, with its postholes and hearths, more potsherds, and maybe a handaxe or two.

Off the Beeline Highway an hour's drive from Phoenix the Ballantine Canyon trail heads into some remarkably rugged country. There is a stream there that flows after the winter rains, but it may have been permanent in previous centuries. Even so, the area looks most unpromising to an organic gardener. There is only a little flat ground near the stream and a great abundance of rocks. Six miles up the trail, the narrow canyon housed a hamlet; some building foundations are outlined in stone walls a foot or two high. Red and grey-brown potsherds lie among the gravel and weeds. A broken metate of volcanic pumice rests in a corner of an old hut where Indian women used it to grind corn during the life of the settlement. How many generations of people made a living in this canyon, with its insignificant brook and an algae-filled spring seeping from the south-facing slope above the village? From my reading and from conversations with archaeologist Glen Rice at Arizona State, I gather that the occupants of this tiny village may or may not have been Hohokam. Although their main population centers were close to the rivers and major streams to the south, there were periods when the Hohokam pushed north; and the Ballantine Canyon village may have been established during one of those times. Alternatively, it is possible that the people who lived there came in from the east, making the village an outlier of the Salado culture. Or perhaps this was a Sinagua site, populated by pioneers from a group that was centered to the north around what is now Flagstaff. Whoever lived in Ballantine Canyon was there when the Phoenix area was occupied by the Hohokam and they almost certainly exchanged goods with the lowland people, possibly trading wood and minerals for beans and corn and specialty items from Mexico.

There is a hint that the Hohokam in the lowland and some groups in the upland desert did not always interact in a friendly manner. Some archaeologists believe they have found "forts" on hilltops in the zone of overlap between low-desert Hohokam and groups resident in the hills. These crude stone fortifications were built late in the period of expansion, shortly before the Hohokam people pulled back out of the mesas and canyons to the north of Phoenix and retreated to the main population centers near the Salt and Gila rivers.

These major sites may have entered a period of decline about this time (1100 A.D.), but the Hohokam persisted until the middle of the fifteenth century before their villages and fields were completely abandoned and the creosote bush and palo verde reclaimed the desert. Perhaps a combination of factors contributed to the end of Hohokam culture, with drought and salinization reducing the agricultural productivity of their irrigated fields, followed by fighting and political turmoil among hungry, desperate groups, struggles that eliminated the broad web of cooperation needed to run the vast irrigation system along the Gila and Salt rivers.

In any case, the adobe walls of the Hohokam gradually melted over hundreds of monsoon cycles. The Indians' durable potsherds were buried in debris and silt, to be uncovered centuries later when the soil that concealed them was washed away in new patterns of erosion or when round-tailed ground squirrels carried them to the surface in the course of excavating burrows in what once were Hohokam households.

But the Hohokam disappeared. Their name, given them by the Pima Indians who followed the Hohokam in the desert, means "all used up," a phrase that might also be applied to the farmland they left behind, if, as some think, it had lost the ability to support a desert culture that had endured for nearly two millennia. Will our culture, so dedicated to using up the land, the water, and the air of our desert Southwest, last half as long as the Hohokam?

July Evening

Halfway to Usery Peak an exquisite collection of lichens grows on a rock by the trail. A deep chartreuse patch borders two colonies of burnt orange, each twice the size of a silver dollar. On the edges of these lichens some blue-green species line up along vertical cracks in the rock, the whole aggregation producing a natural Miro. The colors of the lichens express themselves fully in the soft shade of late afternoon.

On top the sun goes down by degrees in the west. As it descends, the illuminated haze and unlighted shadows behind the isolated hills to the north of Phoenix and beyond create a world in which humans might not exist.

In the east only one mammoth cloud floats among a few sad wisps and sheets of grey in the infinite blue of the evening sky.

A canyon wren works its way up a line of boulders that reaches the top of the mountain. The neatly dressed bird scampers over the rocks, peering into crannies, ducking into alcoves, plucking minute prey from the rough surfaces of the rocks with its decurved bill. Upon reaching the uppermost rock the wren drops suddenly to the ground, sending a small lizard sprinting unnecessarily for cover. The bird turns its head to inspect the earth before mounting the vertical face of the boulder in front of it, moving upward with the skill of a lifetime rock climber, its clawed feet making the most of each irregularity in the wall.

A turkey vulture swings along the ridgetop heading for a more distant peak on the mountain. As the bird approaches the roost, it dives down at an angle before rising to land on a bare rocky perch. Just before touching down, the vulture pulls its black wings in toward its black body with a shudder, like an umbrella collapsed as its owner approaches a doorstep. From its bouldertop the vulture observes a world in transition.

Mimics, Aggressive and Otherwise

I t is the season of the robberflies. In a palo verde on Usery Peak three orange robberflies bumble through the branch tips to perch on bent legs that seem far too long for their bodies. Members of this species will occupy the tree for a few short weeks, their flight season squeezed into a niche in July and August. They are part of a succession of insects that began in late February; since that time, everything from tiny midges to giant tarantula hawk wasps have come to the hilltops according to schedule to wait for sexual partners or to feed on the species that rendezvous here.

Robberflies are killers. They ambush their insect prey, darting out from a perch to grasp a victim with their hairy legs. After stabbing it with its stiletto mouthparts, the predatory fly slowly drains the subdued prey of its internal contents, then drops the husk of its meal to the ground. One of the orange robberflies dangles from a branch, suspended by its front legs, while it consumes a small black bee that droops at the end of the fly's piercing proboscis.

The orange robberfly is only one of about a thousand North American members of its family, the Asilidae. The wonderful thing about insects is the diversity in body form and behavior that has arisen among related species, a diversity that often overshadows that found in comparable assemblages of vertebrates. Robberflies are delightfully diverse. They come in all sizes and colors, from those a few millimeters long to giants (for flies) as long as your thumb. Variation in body size is paralleled in variety of diet. The tiny robberflies swoop after minute midges or delicate true bugs; the biggest species embrace and kill big, chunky grasshoppers or robust bumblebees, incapacitating their hefty targets with lethal injections of saliva.

At the peak of the robberfly flight season, representatives of several species coexist on Usery Peak. In addition to the clownish long-legged orange fly, there are other grey-black asilids, with long, sleek, tapering abdomens. Many of these superficially drab animals have patches of silvery white at the tips of their bodies or streaking their abdomens, so that when they fly up light flashes from them. A much more showy asilid, about the length of my thumbnail, sometimes perches in the palo verdes with its larger cousins. This fly's most striking feature is its brilliant green eyes. Golden brown hairs coat its thorax, and its robust, darker abdomen is banded by rings of pale tan hairs. Backlighted on its perch, the creature assumes a radiance not usually associated with flies. One member of the genus has been

An asilid robberfly feasts on a small desert bee.

given a name that might apply to all its close relatives, *Mallophorina pulchra*, the beautiful *Mallophorina*.

When the Usery Peak *Mallophorina* leaves one perch to go to another or to zip after a potential victim, its golden hairs, posture in flight, and buzzing wings combine to create the illusion that it is a small bee. A great many asilids resemble various species of bees and wasps, and entomologists early on recognized that these mimetic robberflies generally specialized in the dispatch of bees and wasps. *Mallophorina* is a fairly small asilid, and it usually captures small to medium-sized solitary bees, of which some manage a living even in July in the Sonoran Desert. Other, much larger asilids elsewhere look very much like paper wasps or bumblebees, and these hefty predators typically hunt and kill their look-alikes.

The pioneering American entomologist C. V. Riley suggested that the bee- and wasp-mimicking flies were "aggressive mimics" that used their mimicry to approach their victims closely without alarming them. A "bumblebee" asilid might, according to this hypothesis, be able to practice a kind of wolf-in-bee's-clothing tactic, the better to approach and grasp bumblebees, its favored meals. The resemblance of *Mallophorina* to certain small desert bees would constitute aggressive mimicry if these bees were more likely to ignore the fly than some other predatory insect enemies.

The aggressive mimicry hypothesis is an intriguing one, but it has not been tested with asilids and their prey, and there are reasons to think such tests would lead to rejection of the hypothesis. E. B. Poulton pointed out in 1904 that asilids almost never approach their prey stealthily or casually, but instead launch short, rapid attacks from perches in the areas where their prey are flying. The nature of these ambushes is such that a resemblance to the victim would hardly advance the success of the attacker.

Thus it seems likely that the bee- and wasp-mimicking robberflies are engaged in what is called Batesian mimicry, after Henry Bates, the English lepidopterist who first proposed that an edible species could gain some protection from its predators by resembling another species that is noxious, poisonous, or stinging. Birds relish flies but are less fond of stinging Hymenoptera, and with good reason; a flycatcher stung in its mouth by a bumblebee or paper wasp receives a huge dose of toxin relative to its weight and can be expected to suffer proportionally. Humans quickly learn to avoid bees and wasps by their color patterns. Insect-eating birds are equally adept at this form of learning, as many experiments have shown. Because bumblebee-hunting asilids occur by necessity in habitats with their prey, birds that have learned through unhappy experience that bumblebees should be left to their own devices may mistakenly also ignore mimetic stingless asilids, which fool their predators.

Batesian mimics rely on deceit to gain a survival advantage. Their trick can work only on "educated" predators, those that have had an unpleasant encounter or two with a genuinely protected species before they come across the mimic. As a general rule, therefore, Batesian mimics are rare relative to their models, a rule that holds for bee-mimicking robberflies. In addition, as G. P. Waldbauer of the University of Illinois has documented for an extensive array of mimetic flies, the deceiving species usually emerge as adults later in the season than do their models. This scheduling tactic gives local bird predators, particularly the young of the year, an opportunity to sample models and get stung or sick before the mimics appear on the scene.

It is possible that the timing of adulthood in *Mallophorina* has been shaped by bird predation, with the fly coming out only after fledgling flycatchers have tried, with unhappy but highly educational consequences, to eat some small stinging bees. On the other hand, it is just as likely that the mimetic robberfly metamorphoses to adulthood slightly later than its bee models because it would be disastrous for a bee hunter to emerge before there were bees to hunt.

A more probable (but still uncertain) case of adaptive developmental scheduling by a mimetic fly on my study site involves a mydid fly, *Mydas ventralis*. This species belongs to a family, the Mydidae, that is closely allied with the Asilidae. They not only look rather like some asilids, they may also employ the asilid tactic of ambushing insect prey. This family, however, does not contain a great diversity of species; there are less than five hundred species worldwide and only about fifty in the United States. The low number of species, the rarity of those that do exist, and their preference for "the hottest climates at the hottest times of the year" have combined to make mydid flies one of the least-studied of dipterans. Indeed, Frank Cole philosophizes in his *Flies of Western North America* that "like many large and ungainly creatures, they have probably found it difficult to survive in a highly competitive world." Simple

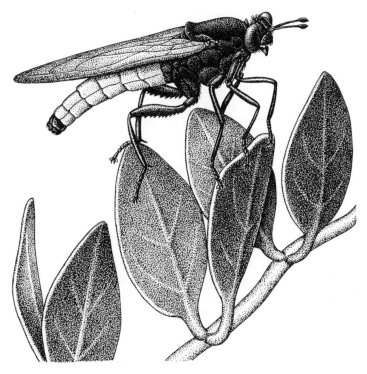

A mydid fly perches on a hilltop jojoba.

accidents of evolutionary history could be responsible for the rarity of mydid flies, of course, but it is true that they are large; indeed, the largest of all flies is a Brazilian mydid, *Mydas heros*, which has a wingspan of four inches. This must be a formidable-looking fly, although adults of this species apparently are actually among the Ferdinands of the mydid world; they feed on nectar, not insect prey.

When I see *Mydas ventralis* on Usery Peak in June and July, however, the flies are not sipping flower nectar or the juices of insect prey, but instead are looking for mates. Like many of their insect predecessors on the local peaktops, males gather on the ridge to secure perch territories where they wait for a female to show up and copulate. One of the species in this group that precedes the mydid to the peaks is a big tarantula hawk wasp whose males claim palo verdes, creosotes, and jojoba bushes as their territories. Male tarantula hawks fly about in conspicuous patrols, showing off their jet-black bodies and bright, red-brown wings. Female tarantula hawks have immense stingers and even the stingless males appear to possess some chemical protection; ash-throated flycatchers never seem to attempt to capture them, despite numerous opportunities. The males smell unpleasantly acrid, and so I suspect they are not tasty morsels.

The flight season of the wasp peaks in May and peters out in June, giving fledgling flycatchers ample time to make a mistake and grab a tarantula hawk or two before the mydid flies come to the ridgetops. These flies, which are just as big as tarantula hawks, do a wonderful imitation of the wasp, but only when they are flying. Although they have dark wings and a red abdomen, rather than red wings and a dark abdomen, when circling their territories they maneuver in a dipping, tilting flight that closely matches that of tarantula hawk wasps. Presumably, it is when it is flying that a mydid fly — or an asilid, for that matter — is at special risk of detection and attack by those birds that ambush insect prey. If juvenile ash-throated flycatchers do sometimes sample a tarantula hawk, only to find it repellent, they might be prone to look the other way when they see a *Mydas ventralis* looping about its peaktop territory. Today, in a truly hot place at the hottest time of the year, there are no flycatchers on Usery Peak, no birds at all, no thought of rain, only a few mydid flies and dormant brittlebushes, and a grey robberfly grimly clutching a skeletal creosote limb.

August

All day the tension has been building. The humidity has been increasing, too, and the ocotillos and ironwoods seem bowed under the weight of the oppressive air. By late afternoon a long line of giant cumulus clouds has formed to the east of Usery Peak and the wind has begun to spin in flickering gusts across the ridge, drawing the still-growing clouds closer to the mountains. As they come, the day darkens. To the south, in the few remaining agricultural fields of Mesa, a reddish brown wall of dust picks itself up and begins to roll sedately to the west. The wall builds, spreading over a great sweep of flatland. In town the introduced palm trees whip themselves into a frenzy, sending bits of frond and fruiting stalks skittering down gritty sidewalks and across lawns.

A few plump drops of rain smack into the bone-dry gravel on the ridge, producing dark stains on the pale ground. A sheet of rain drops out of the sky and advances to the accompaniment of thunder and lightning. A bolt cracks down as rain finally comes back to the mountain, soaking the ground and cleansing the air. The palo verdes shake in the wind, their thin branches striking together, impelled by the force of the thunderstorm. Water courses down the smooth green trunk of a ridgetop palo verde and over the wrinkles at its base to spill out on the ground among the remains of old seed pods that lie brown, cracked, and empty under the tree.

Flying in the Rain

The wonderful storm of a few days ago has reorganized the hillside slightly, cutting little gullies in the steepest parts, depositing fans of gravel in the flatter parts of the trail, carrying the seeds of broom-rape into microscopic cavities in the earth. And the monsoon continues. Along a ridge in the Usery Mountains an isolated shower descends from a dark pool of clouds to the north. As the clouds drift eastward the curtain of rain is pulled slowly to the side, revealing Four Peaks again. Through the haze, with the sun low on the horizon and shining faintly through the showers, the mountains appear greyer than usual and washed of all detail.

An adventurous harvester ant has slipped up one khaki pant leg on a mission of exploration before becoming trapped by the cloth against my thigh. The constrained ant lets me have it, gripping my skin firmly with its jaws, the better to drive the stinger at the tip of her abdomen deeply into my flesh. A second or two is required to appreciate the sting fully, and then I yelp in pain while simultaneously attempting to grab and crush the insect through the cloth of my trousers. The ant has succeeded in giving me a decent injection, and for the rest of the morning a subcutaneous ache accompanies my every move.

The worker ant's suicide mission is related to the nuptial season for desert ants. An ant colony is composed largely of nonreproducing workers, often the daughters of a single fertile queen that founded the self-contained society. But each year there is a time when queens lay eggs that become sons and daughters capable of reproducing, instead of sterile female workers. When the reproductives are mature, they are typically held in their natal nests until an opportune time arises for them to leave. For many desert species, the trigger for mating flights appears to be rainfall, which stimulates the sterile worker ants to pull their reproducing brothers and sisters out into a world made more suitable for colonization by the monsoon.

Of the ants on Usery Ridge, *Pogonomyrmex* harvester ants are the most numerous and conspicuous. Their large, eager-to-sting workers become especially aggressive in defense of their brothers and sisters, which they usher onto the surface after a shower. Once there, the assembled reproductives may surge back into the nest briefly and then out again. Eventually, the ever-increasing mass of alate (winged) reproductives spills out in a frenzied group onto nearby rocks and tufts of sun-dried vegetation. On delicate wings they fly up into the hothouse atmosphere. The wingless workers remain earthbound, touchily guarding the nest and any of their reproductively capable brothers and sisters that remain; these may venture forth later in the monsoon season.

Alates from many different colonies have descended upon a creosote bush on a peaktop. The males scramble frantically up and down the stems of the bush, which gradually acquires a seething cloak of red-winged ants. When I come to the creosote and look down upon it, incoming ants transfer their attention to me, landing on my hat in numbers before I retreat to a lower observation post.

A brief and inconsequential shower passes overhead. The sunshine persists, illuminating the scattered fat raindrops that dive down in a silvery swarm, glittering until they abruptly collide with the earth. I squirm as they splatter coldly against my shirt.

The ants seem to know the shower is transitory and continue about their business. The reproductive forms of many species of ants, including several harvester ants, form mating aggregations on the summits of hills, as well as at other elevated posts, such as tall trees, rooftops, and even chimneys. As males reach such a landmark they secrete a chemical. The sweet-smelling heptanone used by some pogos is a pheromone that attracts still more individuals to the location. When Bert Hölldobler, an accomplished observer of pogos in particular and of ants in general, moved the scent-marked twigs of one landmark tree to a new tree that mate-seeking ants had never used before, the new site quickly lured a host of ants, with many more males than females drawn in by the odor.

Among the common species of harvester ants, the rule is that for every female at a rendezvous point there will be four or five suitors. After releasing their sex pheromone these males scramble over the landmark in a frantic search for one of the relatively rare females. The unbalanced sex ratio ensures that there is intense competition for mates. When a male does find a female, she is usually surrounded by several other males, all of which are struggling to clamber onto her back. The first male to succeed in this endeavor grasps her about the thorax with his mandibles, and then inserts his geni-

Male harvester ants fly to a hilltop mating site as a monsoon shower descends on Four Peaks.

talia. With copulation begun, he releases his mandibular grip and falls back to massage the tip of the female's abdomen with his jaws and front legs. The other males continue to grapple for position on the female, and when the first male disengages — often encouraged by the female, who not so gently bites him — a second and later a third male may have their turns at inseminating the queen. Queens are substantially larger than males, and potentially long-lived. They may be able to store and eventually use sperm from a bevy of partners, accounting for their willingness to copulate with more than one male.

On the other hand, males appear eager to prevent their mates from securing additional partners and more sperm, perhaps because any "extra" sperm decreases the probability that the first male will be the father of offspring produced by that female, should she be so fortunate as to live long enough to create a new generation of reproducing progeny. The efforts of males to monopolize a mate may lead to bizarre consequences. In some cases the male bites the female in half because he is holding her so tightly with his jaws, presumably to prevent other males from prying him off. In turn, queens do the same to some males, perhaps in the course of biting males that refuse to end copulation at the desired moment. When this happens, the tip of the male's abdomen remains attached genitally to his recent partner, thus preventing her from mating again until she can remove the body fragment. Hölldobler wonders whether this outcome might not actually be in the reproductive interest of those males that have succeeded in passing their full sperm load to a female. In essence, the male would have committed a kind of sexual suicide by forcing his mate to kill him. His dismemberment, however, could increase the number of progeny he sires, provided that his attached terminalia prevent the female from mating again but can be removed later by the queen to permit her to lay her eggs, which will be fertilized exclusively by his sperm. Because males that have discharged all their sperm have no way of manufacturing more, there is no reproductive penalty for a male who dies after he has depleted his supply of gametes.

Of course it is also possible that males become separated from their genitalia purely by accident, to neither their advantage nor that of their impatient mates. But the fact that male and female pogos are so quick to use their jaws on each other reminds us that sexual reproduction is not a deliriously harmonious exercise designed for the greater good of the species. Males pull males from females, and females snap at males as individuals seek maximum personal gain in mating aggregations. Males that have failed to inseminate females have left no descendants to carry on their special characteristics; male pogos are endowed with properties that enabled their ancestors to elbow their way to sexual fruition.

Once she has mated as many times as she wishes, unless her wishes are thwarted by the attachment of a portion of her last partner, a queen pogo flies away from the landmark rendezvous area. When she descends to the earth with her sperm storage organs filled to capacity, she immediately makes a final commitment to a terrestrial life by snapping her wings sharply in such a way as to break them off at the base. The dealated ant then scrambles about until she finds a place to dig into the now rain-softened soil; if she succeeds, she will construct a little underground chamber that will be home for the rest of her life. There she quickly lays some eggs that hatch into larval grubs. The queen feeds and cares for her offspring, producing a small band of sterile, wingless daughters. These new workers will assist her in many ways, building a more elaborate and larger nest, gathering food, and tending the next batch of eggs laid by their mother, eggs destined to become still more workers. One incipient colony in thousands will reach the stage at which the female society finally is large enough to support an investment in the generation of alate queens and kings, which will wait until after a monsoon rain to be pushed to the surface to engage in one brief, hectic foray into the daylit world.

A robberfly with an alate ant impaled on its beak perches in a palo verde near the creosote bush. It is two hours since the nuptial frenzy began, and the harvester ants have ceased coming to the bush; indeed, most have now mated and dispersed. A handful of males still wanders in a desultory way among the plant's waxy leaves. The rich aroma of creosote mingles with the scent of *Pogonomyrmex*, signaling a revival in the desert as clearly as does the rainbow that has formed in the thin sheets of rain suspended over Usery Mountain.

The Seasons of the Peccary

A band of white-throated swifts strafes the ridgeline, downing aerial insects in their path. Their scimitar wings slash through the air, whistling as loudly as boys in the back of a school bus. Once they have gone the desert seems unnaturally quiet. In place of the swifts a number of blue-grey dragonflies dart and weave silently through the steamy air, snatching up little black ants on their way to a mating fest in a peaktop palo verde. Whispers come from dragonfly wings as the insects twist and turn in pursuit of their prey.

The silence of the morning is broken by a faint sound, rather like gravel slipping on gravel or dried peas shaken together, coming from the slope just below the ridgeline. The source of the sound is a mystery. Silence suffuses the desert again. And then the noise repeats itself, accompanied by a soft snuffle. A peccary stands in the variegated shade of a palo verde. And another peccary materializes under the tree, before three more move into view, walking upslope from behind a boulder. Two juveniles skitter across a gravelly clearing, prancing and bumping each other as they move toward another cluster of peccaries. An adult female limps sedately past a teddy-bear cholla, one hindfoot bent back at a useless angle. Despite her handicap she seems to have reproduced successfully, because walking almost under her belly is a minute, rabbit-sized baby, stepping daintily forward on the thinnest of legs. Right behind is a second infant of the same size.

Gradually a herd of fourteen peccaries reveals itself, a group composed of animals of all sizes and demeanors, from tentative infants to rambunctious adolescents and dignified adults. The larger javelinas forage under the palo verdes, rooting with their piglike snouts amid the debris beneath the trees. The mysterious noise is a by-product of feeding, the crunches and cracks of processing a tough food, perhaps the rock-hard seeds of palo verdes excavated from shallow caches made by woodrats and pocket mice.

The sociable peccaries orchestrate an erratic symphony of sorts while they snuffle and sniff their way through the litter in search of edibles. When interacting they utter low-pitched grunts and grumbles and high-pitched yips and barks. An overactive youngster bounces into a feeding adult, which whirls around growling; the juvenile squeals loudly as it leaps away.

The band members shift about on the hillside, practicing their various vocalizations, until a few adults begin to walk up toward the saddle. One animal feeding off to the side gives a couple of loud barks. Gradually, in two and threes, the peccaries begin to follow the first individuals to leave, straggling up the hillside and across the saddle. A peccary carries a small joint of staghorn cactus stuck firmly to the ridge of its nose. An adult nuzzles the face of a baby that has paused beside it.

As they pass into the maze of ravines and boulders on the other side one peccary utters an explosive "whoof," as if it had exhaled air sharply through its nose and mouth. The sound of animals run-

A peccary mother with her kit, which was born in time to benefit from the monsoon rains.

ning lasts a few seconds and then all is quiet again. The peccaries have left deep footprints in desert soil softened by last week's rain. Grey, dry feces from previous visits lie scattered on the saddle in a few places, the habitual defecatorium of the herd, which must pass this way regularly.

It is too soon after the start of the monsoon for most desert plants to have responded with new growth that peccaries might harvest, and instead the pigs must make do for awhile with the remnants of the spring burst of productivity. In a short time, however, there will be a late-summer surge of plant growth, and the peccary's breeding pattern in Arizona may reflect this ecological fact. Although peccaries are unusual ungulates in that they can breed year-round, the peak mating season is January and February. Some of the females in the Usery Peak band came into estrus then. Estrous females take an active role in promoting copulation by soliciting the males in their band; a female in heat pushes the partner of her choice and may even mount him or, more oddly, another female. Among cattle, estrous cows may mount other females, too. Geoffrey Parker proposed that when a bull spots a member of his herd being mounted, he hustles over to make sure that a rival male is not inseminating one of "his" females. Once in the vicinity of the female that had been mounting another in the herd, the bull might well be thinking of sexual matters and so would discover that the female was ready, even eager, to mate. Through her ploy the female helps ensure that she will be serviced by a dominant male that may endow her offspring with the attributes associated with a truly dominant individual.

Whether this hypothesis can apply to peccaries is problematic, because no one has established whether dominant males compete with subordinates for receptive females. In any event, most female peccaries become pregnant sometime between January and March. After a five-month gestation period, most births occur between June and August, the heart of the Sonoran Desert summer.

At first glance the typical pattern of reproductive timing in peccaries appears positively masochistic, but the customary reproductive schedule of the animal actually takes into account the effects of the two predictable "rainy" seasons in the desert. Rains in the winter and early spring foster the growth of desert annuals and seed production by desert legumes, especially the palo verdes and ironwoods. The monsoon of late summer rescues and rejuvenates desert plants in August and September. A female that becomes pregnant in February usually will be able to find plenty of food in the spring, when she can build up the caloric reserves that will support the growth of her embryos and later yield milk for her kits, after they are born in the hard days of midsummer. Healthy females can nurse their young for six weeks, so that summer-born babies will not be weaned until mid-August or September, in time to take advantage of plant growth stimulated by the monsoon. These youngsters have a reasonable chance of heading into the winter well nourished.

Peccaries in the Sonoran Desert have to accommodate a complex seasonal schedule of rains, hot weather, and plant growth and dormancy. The pigs do not have much to work with, but they and many other desert organisms often overcome the handicaps that would seem to make survival, let alone reproduction, a highly improbable business. Peccaries and harvester ants, palo verde and brittlebush know all about the seasons of the desert and the delicate highwire act of organizing their lives, not just for their own wellbeing, but for the survival of the offspring that might inherit the desert from them.

August's Saguaro

The saguaro on the hillside looks plumper after having had a chance to collect and store water again. One or two blackened hulls of dried fruits still lie under the bursages beneath the cactus. A little vine has revived and sends fresh tendrils of growth creeping up the west-facing trunk of the saguaro. A minimalist flower, yellow with crinkled petals, shines from within a cluster of reduced leaves.

In the short time since the monsoon began many other desert plants also have begun to celebrate. With soil water levels higher than they have been for months, the ocotillo and fairy duster, the tomatillo and palo verde rush to transpire freely again. All these species have new leaves now, delicate leaves, richly green and moist. The fairy duster, a little perennial shrub, seems particularly transformed with fresh, feathery leaves that would not be out of place on the breast of a tropical pitta or some other jungle bird that lives close to the ground amid green mansions. Collectively, the new greenery has softened the severe tans and greys of the landscape and made the desert seem more hospitable.

The capacity of most desert plants, even little ones like fairy dusters, to effect a miraculous recovery after weeks of baking in the full sun is one of the joys of the desert. But not all species are as tough as the fairy duster, and many die when exposed to the full power of the summer sun. Perhaps surprisingly, the saguaro cactus belongs

A saguaro grows up through the branches of its palo verde nurse tree.

in the sun-sensitive category. Although mature specimens have elephantine hides, baby saguaros do not. Exposure to direct sunlight
often stresses or destroys the delicate growing zone at the top of a
young plant, leading to its premature demise under conditions that
many other Sonoran Desert species tolerate with equanimity.

More than fifty years ago the great desert botanist Forrest Shreve
realized that there is an association between saguaro cactus and
various other plants, especially palo verde trees. The fact that saguaros are found growing under or up through the canopy of palo
verdes and other shrubs far more often than expected by chance

suggested to Shreve that the establishment of a saguaro was dependent on the shelter afforded by "nurse plants." The diffuse cover provided by a palo verde or other nurse plant evidently prevents overheating (and may also reduce the risk of frost damage during winter cold spells).

There are alternative hypotheses to account for the close physical proximity between so many saguaros and sheltering shrubs. For example, it may be that the consumers of saguaro fruits, such as woodrats and white-winged doves, spend more time in the shade of palo verdes than elsewhere. As rats and doves digest saguaro fruit and produce seedy feces, their droppings will be deposited primarily beneath the plants that shelter them. Such a pattern would lead incidentally to a correlation between the distribution of saguaros and certain trees and shrubs.

Nevertheless, there is no doubt that young saguaros are damaged by intense sunlight. The fact that small saguaros less than a half-meter in height are almost never found out in the open or beneath dead (canopyless) trees suggests that leafy cover is vital for the survival of young saguaros. Let us accept, therefore, that the association between saguaros and palo verdes arises because the cactus really does benefit from the arrangement. But do palo verdes gain or lose anything by "helping" saguaros become established?

The label "nurse plants" tempts us to think that the interaction between palo verde and saguaro is a benign one, part of some beneficent scheme of Mother Nature. And it could be so, provided the presence of the saguaro also benefited the nurse tree or at least did not harm it. Joseph McAuliffe has demonstrated, however, that saguaros are far from kind to their nurses. He measured the vigor of palo verdes relative to their proximity to saguaro cacti in a study plot in Organ Pipe Cactus National Monument. Nurse trees there had far more dead branches and twigs than did trees that were not sheltering a saguaro. Not only were palo verdes next to saguaros less healthy, many of them were flat-out dead, moribund, finished. More than sixty percent of nurse trees with trunk diameters in excess of twenty centimeters had died, whereas only about fifteen percent of similar-sized palo verdes without saguaro neighbors were dead in McAuliffe's study site.

These results show convincingly that when a saguaro takes root beneath a palo verde the tree is probably destined for gradual decline and relatively early death. The disastrous consequences of nursing a saguaro almost certainly stem from the ability of the cactus to put out a network of shallow roots that intercept water that would otherwise percolate down to the deeper root systems of palo verdes. As it grows, the saguaro's root umbrella subjects its nurse tree to increasing water stress, leading first to stem die-back as the palo verde automatically prunes itself, removing some of its water-transpiring surface area. Eventually, however, even the drastic remedy of self-amputation fails, and the tree dies.

In turn, adult saguaros become "nurse plants" by sheltering some desert birds, especially gila woodpeckers and gilded flickers, both of which excavate nest cavities in the flesh of the giant cactus. Just as palo verdes can do nothing about the establishment of saguaro seedlings in their domain, there is little a saguaro can do when it is beset by hammering woodpeckers intent on sculpting a nest site in its flesh. Saguaros try to limit the damage by sealing off the wound with thick scar tissue, which helps prevent the cactus from becoming infected with killer bacteria.

McAuliffe, a true aficionado of saguaro biology, examined the distribution of nests built by the medium-sized gila woodpeckers and the larger gilded flickers. He and a coworker, Paul Hendricks, found a rather odd result, which was that the smaller woodpecker tended to nest lower on saguaros, where trunks and arms are thicker, whereas the larger flicker typically located its nests in the thinner top three meters of stem. Because flickers have to build a larger nest cavity than do gila woodpeckers, one would have guessed that they should prefer thicker parts of saguaros; perhaps flickers are excluded from these locations by the gila woodpecker.

The competitive exclusion hypothesis can be tested by looking at the distribution of flicker nests in saguaros with and without the potential competitor. Such a test shows that gilded flickers do not shift their nest sites downward when they have exclusive control of a cactus. So much for the idea that competitive interaction with woodpeckers determines where the gilded flicker constructs its nests.

McAuliffe and Hendricks have offered an alternative explanation, which is that the relatively delicate, narrow bill of the gilded flicker limits sites at which it can excavate a cavity sufficiently large to accommodate a hefty incubating adult and a brood of youngsters. In order to create such a nest, flickers must cut through the ring of woody rods that lies under the outer fleshy cortex and constitutes the internal skeleton of the saguaro. These rods are thick and tough except in the upper parts of saguaro stems, where they become thinner and weaker. By cutting into a saguaro near the apex of a stem a flicker saves itself considerable effort and wear and tear on its thin beak.

The smaller but stouter-billed gila woodpecker needs a smaller nest cavity, one that can be accommodated entirely within the relatively soft, fleshy outer cortex in places where the cortex is relatively thick, namely the lower sections of trunks and arms. There the woodpecker chops its way easily through to the skeletal rods, which it uses as the back wall of its nest chamber, rather than attempting to chisel through them. As a result of its need for less space, the gila woodpecker can nest lower on saguaros than can gilded flickers.

Gila woodpeckers damage saguaros relatively little when they nest within the cortex, whose primary function for the cactus is to store water. The woodpecker tosses out a small amount of water-storing tissue, the cactus seals off the wound, and that is that. In contrast, the gilded flicker is to a saguaro as a saguaro is to a nurse tree. By severing some or all of the skeletal rods at the tip of an arm or trunk the flicker weakens the stem apex, creating for the cactus the grave risk of decapitation. The loss of an arm tip occurs most often during the high winds that accompany violent summer thunderstorms. If the severed arm or trunk tip is not promptly sealed off with scar tissue the cactus risks infection and subsequent saguaro rot, a process that can reduce it to a brown statue of decay in remarkably short order.

The likelihood that gilded flickers are unwitting executioners of saguaros is high; flicker nests occur in about twenty percent of all large dead saguaros (in McAuliffe's sample), but in only five percent of living saguaros of similar dimensions. Cacti imposed upon by nesting flickers therefore have rates of mortality far higher than do those that escape the attention of a breeding pair. In contrast, the nest cavities of gila woodpeckers do not occur in dead saguaros in higher frequency than in samples of living cacti. The plant can nurse a gila woodpecker's nest with little or no effect on its survival.

The interactions between saguaro and nurse tree and between gilded flicker and giant cactus reveal how subtle the damaging consequences of associations between species can be. The success of one individual often depends directly on the demise of another, and even when the relationship is not instantly deadly it can be insidiously lethal. This fact should sober those who are eager to ascribe harmony to nature.

High on the arm of a saguaro a gilded flicker harmonizes with the wind, its staccato call ringing through a forest of the giant cacti. If only the palo verdes could hear, perhaps they would take heart.

A Wolf in Vulture's Clothing

After a temporary break in the monsoon a new moist air mass has wedged itself into Arizona. The humidity has increased daily over the last few days, until today a nearly suffocating band of grey clouds blankets the earth. Perhaps this much moisture in the air means that rain is on the way, but there is no guarantee of that in the desert.

A few orange robberflies are still in the palo verdes, bumping each other as they circle through the thin green twigs of the trees, and there is a delightful bumblebee-mimicking robberfly as well, yellow and black, but not looking much like a bumblebee until it flies out from its perch.

Two brown towhees tumble down the hillside, chasing each other through the dried scrub vegetation, their squeals of excitement seeming entirely out of place in the sullen atmosphere.

A light wind pushes thick clouds across the sky, and far to the south a sheet of rain hangs suspended in midair, the streamers evaporating before they reach the ground. A few turkey vultures ride the wind as they soar along the backbone of the ridge. One of the vultures looks slightly different. Although it holds its black wings at an upward slant without a single flap, as a good turkey vulture should, there is something just a bit odd about it.

It drifts down the ridge, tilting slightly from side to side, offering a clearer and clearer view. There is a neatness about the bird, a trimness that is *not* characteristic of turkey vultures. That's because it is not a turkey vulture but a zone-tailed hawk, a fact that becomes clear at last when the hawk glides past to reveal the distinctive white band on its tail.

I have never identified a zone-tailed hawk before in the Usery Mountains, but perhaps I have been fooled before by the hawk's close resemblance to a turkey vulture. It is hard to believe that the resemblance is purely accidental, given the closeness of the match between the appearances and behaviors of the two species.

But which species is the mimic? Over evolutionary time the zone-tailed hawk had to be the one that changed, gradually evolving looks and flight pattern that matched those of the vulture. Turkey vultures are vastly more common and widespread than are zone-tailed hawks. Given that vultures occur in many regions from which the hawk is absent, vultures are unlikely to mimic a species that occupies only a small part of their range.

How might such a mimicry have come about? The zone-tailed hawk is a member of the genus *Buteo*, a group whose members usually have broad wings and broad tails and who soar far above the ground in thermal updrafts with their wings held flat. Unlike its close relatives, however, the zone-tailed hawk has narrow wings and a long narrow tail like the turkey vulture. It is the only *Buteo* whose adults and young are always decked out in funereal black plumage. Moreover, it soars closer to the ground than do most other hawks in its genus, holding its wings in a V as does a turkey vulture.

Helmut Mueller points out that there are trade-offs in any wing designed to achieve soaring flight. The typical *Buteo* pattern maximizes the lift to be gained from the wing surface of the bird, but this benefit is purchased at the price of a loss of stability. Should wind fluctuations lift one wing more than the other, the bird will begin to roll, to lose altitude, and to lose control altogether unless it adjusts quickly to equalize lift on both wings. A bird that holds its wings at a dihedral in the manner of turkey vultures sacrifices lift but gains stability. Because of the aerodynamics of wings held in a slight V, incipient rolls are automatically corrected.

Mueller proposes that those hawks and vultures that soar relatively near the ground probably encounter more variable wind conditions than do those that ride thermals to higher heights. Frequent fluctuations in wind velocity constantly threaten to send a soarer into a costly roll, and so require continual adjustments of wing position, unless the bird uses the trick of holding the wings at a dihedral. In support of this aerodynamic argument Mueller notes that all harriers, including the familiar marsh harrier, soar close to the ground and that all employ the wings-tilted-slightly-up tactic.

But what does a zone-tailed hawk gain in terms of descendant-leaving power by soaring close to the ground like a turkey vulture? Edwin Willis suggests that the prey of the hawk become habituated to turkey vultures, which are harmless scavengers. Given the abundance of inoffensive vultures, it pays rock squirrels, lizards, and small birds (the prey of zone-tails) to ignore carrion-eaters rather than dashing for cover each time a vulture floats above them. A zone-tailed hawk operating in a neighborhood with sufficient turkey vultures takes advantage, so the argument goes, of the indifference with which habituated prey treat soaring vultures. The hawk can use its looks to get close enough to attack its victims, which sometimes do not catch on until it is much too late.

Willis notes that zone-tailed hawks are everywhere scarcer than their vulture "models," enabling prey to become habituated to soaring objects that looked like vultures. Furthermore, zone-tails almost always travel in the company of vultures; when the hawk is soaring like a vulture, prey species beneath appear unconcerned and unalert to danger. Willis has observed only one attack by a soaring pseudo-vulture, which suddenly dove straight down in an apparent attempt to capture a marsh bird below it. In this case the hawk failed, but the zone-tail's behavior suggested that it might get closer to some victims by looking like a vulture before shooting down onto the surprised prey. Here we have a possible case of aggressive mimicry that may hold up, although the idea has yet to be tested thoroughly. If it were shown that the zone-tailed hawk's appearance really deceives its prey, it would be one of only a few "pure" cases of visual aggressive mimicry. In most instances the resemblance of a predator to something harmless clearly serves a dual function. For example, those tropical flower mantids that look exactly like parts of the brightly colored flowers on which they perch in ambush may avoid detection both by their prey and by their predators.

The cryptic leaf fish of South America, which looks and behaves like a dead leaf floating in the current, apparently is able to slip up on unsuspecting prey by virtue of its deceit; however, it also is likely to be overlooked by the kingfishers and others that would be happy to consume it if they realized it was a fish, rather than thinking of it as a leaf.

Another example of this kind is provided by an assassin bug that lives in termite colonies and feeds on the inhabitants. Termites generally are good at recognizing invaders (which do not smell the

The zone-tailed hawk (below) closely resembles the turkey vulture (above) in both plumage and flight behavior.

same as they do) and dispatching them. The crafty assassin bug thwarts the termite's intruder recognition system by taking the husks of its victims, after having drained them of their internal fluids, and attaching them to its back. After a time the predator can march about with impunity, concealed under a mound of empty termite corpses that possess the colony's special chemical badge. Here too, however, aggressive mimicry probably combines with deception of the assassin bug's predators, whatever these might be, because they are unlikely to recognize it for what it is under its cloak of disguise.

I do not believe that zone-tailed hawks have predators that could be persuaded to avoid them because of their resemblance to turkey vultures. Their mimicry, if that is what it is, can only serve a predatory purpose.

The zone-tailed hawk sails away from Usery Peak in the company of a small pod of turkey vultures. They head across the wide gap cut by the Salt River toward Red Mountain, where they will scan the terrain for their different kinds of meals. The first cumulus clouds of the day mushroom over Four Peaks, floating above the mountains with a stability that turkey vultures and zone-tailed hawks cannot hope to match.

August Afternoon

The sun stares at Usery Mountain. The air on the mountain has an alkaline taste, a smothering touch, a faint scent of creosote. In the Goldfields Mountains across the great basin parallel lines of golden sandstone provide the last, temporary accent in a landscape surrendering unconditionally to muted greys and purples. Black shadows of two distant clouds creep almost imperceptibly across the sombre desert. A monsoon cloud boils slowly, whitely over the Goldfields.

The wind flares for a moment. Two branches in a palo verde rub together with careless squeaks.

A gunshot far to the left and below. And then another.

Lost on the farthest horizon, the sketchy line of a mountain ridge barely marks the boundary of an oceanic sky, the colors of earth and atmosphere merging.

Creosote grasshoppers sing their marginal songs. The giant cumulus climbs higher and higher, scaling the ladder from the pale bottom of the sky to the pure cerulean blues on the ceiling of the world.

A flurry of gunfire. An answering rattle of grasshopper ticks. A breeze slips among the green twigs of the palo verdes, shaking them awake with earnest conversation.

Carotenoids Make the Man

In a palo verde on Usery Mountain a big black robberfly feasts on a member of its own species. The cannibal straddles its victim in what seems at first to be a sexual pose; actually, the upper fly has inserted its piercing mouthparts into the thorax of its deceased companion.

A few cicadas sing on the hillside. Their collective song sounds like a vibrating wire, a song that slices through the humidified air of midmorning. On the ridgetop a small but elegant lizard sprints from rock to rock, looking dry and neat on this sultry day. At each rock perch the lizard stops to perform a series of rapid push-ups, as if to emphasize its independence from the climate that reduces mammals to inactivity. The lizard's sleek body is adorned largely with desert greys and browns, forming the canvas for white stripes and neat orange dots painted brightly along its sides. In addition, the animal possesses a striking azure-blue patch on either side of its belly near its hindlegs. Another less strikingly colored lizard of the same species slips from bush to bush in a path parallel to that taken by the push-up performer.

Only adult male greater earless lizards are endowed with large numbers of brilliant orange spots. When males run through their push-up displays they apparently are threatening rival males or advertising themselves to nearby females. But to what purpose? Is a male's success in attracting a female's attention in any way influ-

Male greater earless lizards bear bright orange spots that may signal something important to females intent on choosing a mate.

enced by his color pattern, and particularly by the orange spots and blue patch that stand out so beautifully on his skin? Researchers studying other animals have found that a female's choice of mate may depend on the male's color. For example, Astrid Kodric-Brown has studied female choice in the guppy, a little fish whose males also have spots of color on their bodies; some spots are red or yellow, others blue-green or white. Male guppies perform an energetic courtship featuring much tail-waving, body vibration and assorted display. During male courtship females have the opportunity to inspect their potential partners closely. Because male guppies cannot force females to mate with them, females would appear to be free to choose among courting males, which often display to females in the company of rivals.

Kodric-Brown asked whether color might play a role in a female's preference for a particular male. To answer her question, she paired male guppies with different color patterns in a three-compartmented aquarium. In the central chamber a female was positioned to observe two males, one in the right-hand compartment and the other in the left. Males were matched in size and for the rate at which they produced courtship displays, so that any preference for a male would have to be based on his coloration and not on his behavior *per se.*

Kodric-Brown found that her female guppies often spent eighty percent or more of their time within a few inches of one of the two males during two trials. Typically, the preferred male was one whose color pattern featured red or yellow spots. But why should these particular colors be so important to females when the amount of blue or white pigment apparently does not make a female guppy's heart beat faster?

As Kodric-Brown points out, reds and yellows (and oranges) are carotenoid pigments, chemical substances that fish cannot manufacture themselves and so must instead acquire and sequester from the foods they eat. As a guppy locates small insects and consumes them it stores the small amounts of carotenoids in these foods and uses them to colorize its body. Thus the amount of carotenoid pigments on a guppy's body provides a visual history of his past foraging experience. Males that are successful finders and consumers of insects will be able to show off lots of carotenoids, but those that have had a difficult time finding high-protein food will not. Perhaps only some males have the "good" genes needed to develop superior foraging skills; if so, only those males will have bright carotenoid colors, and females that prefer them will have offspring that carry their partners' good genes.

The hypothesis that female choice has influenced the evolution of male attributes, favoring those that honestly signal something about their abilities and genetic features, is controversial. Although the idea is far from universally accepted by evolutionary biologists, it is a start. The good genes hypothesis helps us look at earless lizards with a question or two that we would not have otherwise.

For example, if the argument is right, males of the greater earless lizard should vary in the number or size of their orange dots in ways that reflect their feeding history or some other attribute that correlates with their physical condition and capabilities. Are the lizard's orange pigments carotenes? William Cooper of Auburn University reports that the bright yellows and oranges of a close relative of the greater earless lizard are *not* produced primarily by carotenes. Another class of chemicals, pteridines, are largely responsible for the cheerful colors of this cousin, the keeled earless lizard. Probably the same is true for the greater earless lizard, but it would still be possible for the source of pteridines to be the animal's foods, in which case these substances could act as markers of food intake. Cooper has yet to learn whether "his" lizard manufactures the orange pteridine pigments from scratch or ingests and recycles them.

Let us assume that the orange dots on males of the greater earless lizard contain information about an individual's feeding history. Do females pay any attention to this information? One of the few studies on the sensitivity of female lizards to the color of their mates was done by David Crews, now at the University of Texas, in an experiment with the green anole of the southeastern United States. Males of this slim little lizard can distend the skin on their throats, the dewlap, pushing it out to create a rigid semicircular wafer of skin, which is bright red in mature adults. If, however, the dewlap is injected with India ink it becomes blue when the male erects this body part in front of observant females. In Crews's experiment female anoles exposed to males with a blue dewlap were just as likely to experience ovarian growth, a precondition for becoming sexually active, as were females that saw a normal red-dewlapped male.

The enhanced development of the ovaries of females exposed to blue dewlaps casts something of a pall over the color-as-a-basis-for-female-choice hypothesis, but perhaps we should not abandon the idea entirely after just one negative experiment. Indeed, a subsequent test that employed substantially different procedures succeeded in demonstrating that female anoles given a simultaneous choice between a male with a red dewlap and one with a dewlap painted green overwhelmingly "preferred" the male that signaled with a red flag. Here females were placed in a glass-walled terrarium with a view of two other cages, one containing a normal male and the other a painted individual. The females consistently attempted to crawl or jump toward the cage in which they could see a male flashing his red dewlap. They were not excited by the green-dewlapped male.

This experiment demonstrates that female green anoles apparently are not as obtuse as they have seemed on occasion, but it is one thing to show that they discriminate between red and green dewlaps and another to prove that they are prejudiced in favor of males with brighter red dewlaps over those with paler display structures. Fine discriminations of this sort are precisely what are required if we are to claim that a female lizard can judge a male's genes by the color of his skin.

No one has yet experimentally tested the possible relation between female choice and male color pattern in the greater earless lizard, a fact that seems not to dismay the little lizards on Usery Peak. They zip across the gravel, bob up and down on stiff legs, and keep a close eye on those who seem to admire them for their artful decorations.

A Recommendation for Scorpions

S ince the monsoon has come to central Arizona there have been two thunderstorms and a brief shower in the Usery Mountains. Palo verde seedlings have sprouted from seeds that escaped the peccaries and woodrats. They poke their delicate, leafy green bodies up from the gravel that concealed them from desert seed-eaters.

After the initial storms there has been a long break. On some afternoons recently, magnificent cumulus clouds have pulled themselves together before rumbling into the evening on a journey to one place or another, but not to the Usery Mountains. The ocotillo have begun to drop their once hopeful leaves and the little ferns at the bases of boulders have folded themselves back into a mass of withered brown curls. Some palo verde seedlings droop sadly in terminal water-stress.

On the mountaintop the sky is cleanly blue and cloudless everywhere, except far to the southeast. A gathering of eight turkey vultures dances along the ridgeline and back, arcing in loose ellipses just overhead. As one bird kites by it dangles its pale green chicken legs briefly in the wind before tucking them neatly back under its tail. No vulture seems willing to break from the mountain. It is as if they are waiting for one of their company to pick up enough courage to lead the way, sailing from their sky island to pioneer a vast and uncertain ocean of desert.

A scorpion tucks itself into a little depression in the soil under a rock, where it is insulated from the extreme heat by its stony ceiling. The scorpion stays put, unwilling to move even when its roof is removed. It is small, brown, and inconspicuous, and it carries its stinger-tipped tail curled over its back. I put the rock back, recreating the scorpion's shelter, and leave it in peace.

One summer shortly after we moved to Arizona I walked into the bedroom of the cabin we had rented in the Chiricahua Mountains and found a large pale scorpion perched dead center on the clean white coverlet of the bed. Biologists should be able to deal calmly with all matters biological, but instead I felt a mixture of fear, anger, and disgust at the sight of the scorpion. How dare it sit there as if it owned the place, guaranteeing a small unpleasant uncertainty in my mind whenever I got into bed.

I backed quietly into the next room, retrieved a magazine from the table, fashioned a club of it, and returned to the bedroom to bludgeon the scorpion to death. The deed done, I gingerly disposed of the corpse.

Scorpions have relatively few admirers. Their arched abdomen tip seems a threat, their customary secretiveness is unnerving, and their prehistoric appearance is repellent to most of us. It also is true that scorpions will in self-defense sting humans, leading in some cases to a systemic reaction complete with staggering gait, drooling, abdominal cramps, even convulsions. Not a pretty picture. No wonder then that in scorpion country we shake our shoes out in the morning and do the same with jackets or shirts left hanging on a hook. The thought of slipping a foot into a shoe occupied by a scorpion is disturbing. The cartoonist Gary Larson reminds us, however, that from a scorpion's perspective the thought of being in a shoe into which a human foot is inserted is the stuff of which scorpion nightmares are made.

Now that I have spent a few more years in places where scorpions are part of the landscape I have revised my opinion of them and can take a modest interest in their biology, rather than reacting on murderous impulse whenever I happen to come across one. We lived for a time in a Costa Rican house richly endowed with scorpions; we came eventually to usher them carefully out the front door, as guests who had overstayed their welcome rather than as perpetrators of a capital offense.

In Arizona there is only one scorpion species among many that poses any real threat to human well-being. Ironically, this is one of the smallest species, *Centruroides sculpturatus*, the bark scorpion. Although only a couple of inches long, its venom packs considerable punch and is said to be life-threatening for very young children. Even so, there have been no deaths attributed to scorpion stings in Arizona for more than a decade. The stings of the other thirty or so species found in the state are undeniably painful, but not a cause for major alarm unless one is an insect, the intended target of the sting of most scorpions.

Scorpions, which are adept hunters, catch crickets and the like with pincers on the ends of their first pair of leglike appendages. While holding on, a scorpion jabs the unlucky prey with its stinger, subduing it promptly so that it can be dismembered and consumed. Scorpions also hunt and kill other scorpions. In their study of four species living in the Mojave Desert in California, Gary Polis and Sharon McCormick found scorpions at night feasting on fellow scorpions so often that they decided to explore the phenomenon systematically. They took advantage of a technique for locating scorpions used by the small coterie of researchers in this field, a technique based on the fact that scorpions fluoresce when exposed to ultraviolet light. To locate scorpions at night, therefore, one shines a UV light over the desert floor, and any scorpion struck by the beam will glow to reveal its presence. By tracking scorpions in this way Polis and McCormick discovered that big scorpions do indeed regularly capture smaller ones. In their study areas one large predatory scorpion accounted for five to ten percent of the deaths among several other coexisting species. When they experimentally removed the killer species from desert plots (and their take was more than six thousand in about two-and-a-half years), the smaller species increased substantially in number. Polis and McCormick had demonstrated that the community of scorpion species living together is shaped directly by predation among them.

Scorpions feed not only on members of other species; some species are ardent cannibals. About twenty-five percent of the total biomass consumed by the scorpion *Paururoctonus mesaensis* consists of other individuals of its own species. Members of the smallest size class in the population make up a majority of the victims. Given that large species take advantage of smaller ones, perhaps it is not too surprising that mature adults sometimes kill and eat juveniles of their own species, which are smaller than they are. Small scorpions are safe prey for larger ones, and so the cost of subduing a victim is slight. Moreover, a member of one's own species ought to be a nutritious thing to eat, because its tissues contain the very substances that a conspecific requires for its growth and maintenance. This hypothesis has not been tested with scorpions, but in one study of mosquitofish, which indulge in casual cannibalism, individuals that received dried, minced conspecifics in their diet tended to grow larger or to develop larger gonads. These results were obtained even though the control groups received the same overall amount of food as those receiving meals of their own species. Thus, cannibals may derive a potential reproductive reward for their behavior.

If eating their own kind also fosters better growth in cannibal scorpions, then these animals would have yet another reason to add members of their own species to their diet. So long as a cannibal eats offspring unrelated to it more often than it eats its own progeny or those of close relatives, it will not diminsh the spread of its own genes, a component of which are involved in the development of cannibalistic tendencies in itself and in kin that share these genes.

Because adults of many species are unlikely to eat their own offspring, cannibalism ought to be fairly common; it is. The phenomenon has been reported not just for scorpions, but also for various fishes, frogs, toads, protozoans, rotifers, ground squirrels, spiders and robberflies. Typically, larger members of the species prey upon smaller ones, particularly when other food is scarce and conspecifics are common.

Arguably the most dramatic form of cannibalism involves the consumption of a male by his mate. Sexual cannibalism occurs in scorpions as well as in various other arachnids and insects, of which the most familiar examples are certain spiders and the praying mantis. These cases fit the usual pattern, in that the cannibals tend to be females that are larger than the males they eat. Their size advantage helps females overwhelm their partners, who are forced by their sexual impulses to come courting, which brings them within attack range.

Recently, however, several authors have argued that stories of sexual cannibalism have been overblown or are outright myths, at least for animals living in the wild. It is true that sexual cannibalism in the praying mantis, one of the most widely reported examples of the phenomenon, has been observed almost entirely under laboratory conditions. Eckehard Liske and W. Jack Davis claim that sexual cannibalism in the mantis is essentially an artifact of laboratory conditions. However, Liske and Davis also noted that males of the species they studied (and there are many species that can rightly be called "praying mantises") approached their partners with extreme caution and leaped onto their backs from a considerable distance. As Timothy Birkhead and his collaborators note, it is improbable in the extreme that males would be so nervous and careful if there were no chance that females might do them in.

Various laboratory studies suggest that sexual cannibalism in mantids is related to the nutritional condition of the female. She is far more likely to consume her partner, before, during, or after mating (and all are possible) if she has been underfed. In Birkhead's study, malnourished females that succeeded in polishing off a mate significantly increased the weight of the egg mass they produced, leading to an estimated increment of twenty percent in the number of young they would earn from that breeding attempt. There is little doubt, therefore, that if female mantids were to have a difficult time in securing food under natural conditions, they would improve their reproductive success by supplementing their limited diets with the bodies of their mates.

What has intrigued some evolutionary biologists is the possibility that males also could gain by becoming fodder for a sexual cannibal. If the male fathers the offspring an underfed cannibalistic female produces after a mating that ended in his demise, and the female's fecundity improved twenty percent as a result, the male would enjoy (posthumously) a twenty percent addition to his output of descendants from this female. The question is, could a reproductive benefit of this magnitude compensate for the elimination of any future reproductive attempts with other females? Birkhead's group thinks this is improbable, and so do I, but it all depends on how likely sexual contacts are under field conditions. Old males near the end of their lives that had failed to find females for a long time (because females were scarce) might be better off sacrificing themselves as food to any females they finally located rather than trying to stay alive to search fruitlessly a little longer.

In any case, sexual cannibalism has probably had an effect on the behavior of male mantises subjected to its risk (or benefits), favoring a considerable degree of caution among males when dealing

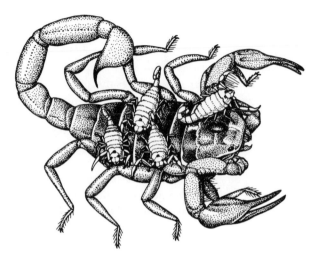

A maternal scorpion carries her brood on her back.

with females. Ordinary garden-variety cannibalism in scorpions also seems likely to have had its evolutionary impact on the behavior of those potentially affected by this form of predation. For example, the existence of cannibal types within a species may be one factor that has contributed to the evolution of maternal behavior in many scorpions. Despite their coldly antediluvian appearance, female scorpions usually are highly solicitous of their newborns, which clamber onto their mother's back. The mound of infants nestles beneath the protective arched tail of the female, whose large size and potent sting probably deter any number of enemies, among them other scorpions, that would gladly include baby scorpions in their diets.

But even mothers become cannibals of their progeny if they are subjected to food stress, presumably because a female's lifetime reproductive success is enhanced by recycling offspring that have little or no chance to reach reproductive age themselves. By eating some offspring that would otherwise starve, a female could increase the probability that she will survive to breed again, perhaps under better conditions that will give her next round of babies a better chance to pass on the genes they have inherited from their mother.

These hypotheses have yet to be tested rigorously in any species of scorpion, but at least they provide a way for future researchers to analyze the facets of cannibalism among these animals.

When I see a scorpion these days I no longer view it in one-dimensional terms, seeing only the stinger of the arachnid and nothing else. Instead I am aware that beneath its seemingly primitive exoskeleton lies the capacity for skillful nighttime hunting, cannibalism, and maternal care. Even the exoskeleton itself becomes a beautiful thing when you learn that it is covered with several wax layers that make the scorpion a nearly watertight machine. Thanks to their impervious cuticles, desert-dwelling scorpions lose water at rates lower than that of any other creature. Moreover, scorpions can tolerate higher body temperatures than can most other desert arthropods. They also can withstand severe dehydration, remaining alive even after having lost forty percent of their body weight, whereas a human that has lost ten percent of his body weight from dehydration is in dire straits. Knowing what I know now, I think I would get little satisfaction these days from clubbing a scorpion into oblivion. On the other hand, they still leave something to be desired as companions in bed.

September

The ironwood in the wash has undergone many changes over the course of the summer. In May it lost most of the leaves on its outer twigs and replaced foliage with flower buds. The buds burst in the first week of June, converting a ratty-looking tree to a plant of exquisite beauty, a temple seemingly composed entirely of radiant red-purple blooms aflame with color in the early morning light. The ironwood sustained its flowers for two weeks, during which it was visited daily by hundreds of digger bee females that harvested the pollen and nectar.

As the flowers were pollinated and set seed, the faded petals dropped to the ground to carpet a circle of sand beneath the tree. Where once flowers bloomed, green seed pods grew, each just large enough to hold a couple of leguminous beans within a slightly furry case. Rock squirrels abandoned their boulder retreats and became arboreal again to pull the ironwood's seeds into their mouths.

By July the green pods had turned mottled brown, then deep chocolate, as the surviving beans matured and dried. The seeds and their covers fell to earth amidst the few remaining grey fragments of flower petals. Woodrats and pocket mice came at night to gather what the peccaries left untouched. The ironwood's outer limbs became bare again, with only a few curled pods dangling from branch tips and a collection of dusty green leaves on its inner arms. The dormant tree had joined the rest of us in waiting for the monsoon.

On this day in early September the ironwood has a new coat of bright green leaves, each one small to minimize water losses; even though it rained in August, water conservation is still the order of the day in the desert. The full outline of the tree has been restored, its symmetry regained.

A zebra-tailed lizard sits at the boundary between the pool of shade under the ironwood and the open white gravel *of the wash. Born during the last few weeks, the zebra-tail is a miniature version of the adults that run on stilted legs through the desert. The elegant, banded tail of the tiny lizard curls over its back and arcs from right to left and back again in a metronomic rhythm. A turkey vulture passes overhead, its travel purposeful, its feathers trim.*

The Cost of Coyote Meat: An Update

Early in the day the gullies are black on the west-facing slope of the ridge. They grow wider as they run down the hillside, draining the mountain's shadows into the big dry wash at its base. Several saguaros raise their arms out of the darkness to touch the sunlight streaming over the ridge.

Far below in the shade, three cactus wrens and a curve-billed thrasher chip and scold in anger and distress. They move slowly up the slope and eventually two coyote cubs, three-quarters grown, come into view, trailing their retinue of mobbing birds. The coyotes travel somewhat apart, yet move together, investigating the desert as they slowly ascend to the ridgeline. They are small animals, with scruffy reddish muzzles and dark tail tips, but they carry themselves with a matter-of-fact dignity, ignoring the mobbing wrens.

At the ridgetop one cub stops to inspect a tomatillo shrub dotted with little red fruits. It begins to snap them off the shrub with its sharp teeth, quickly gathering all those in easy reach. Having depleted the simple harvest, it begins to jump, snatching those higher on the bush.

Coyotes are, like us, extreme omnivores. Little desert fruits and seeds, jackrabbits and cottontails, whiptail lizards, plump domestic lambs and house cats, a farmer's musk melons, all are grist to a coyote's mill. Some coyotes even practice a kind of Earth First! "terrorism" by chewing on and puncturing plastic irrigation piping of the sort used by avocado farmers. Because coyotes can eat almost anything they can live almost anywhere, from the tame farms of Pennsylvania to the wild ranches of Montana, from the empty deserts of Arizona to the chic suburbs of Los Angeles.

The overlap in our ranges and diets clearly contributes to the bad feeling that characterizes human-coyote relations. Although people might not begrudge a coyote its fill of tomatillo fruits, the loss of a sheep or a pronghorn fawn stimulates murderous impulses in many. However, not everyone feels this way. I, for one, find coyotes a good deal more interesting than sheep, and if they kill some game animals too, so be it.

Here in Arizona, with its tradition of ranching and hunting, most people see coyotes as the enemy. The pressure to "do something" about coyotes has been strong enough to cause various state and federal agencies to invest considerable time and energy in an effort to "control" (i.e., kill) coyotes in the state. My colleague Gerald Cole, now retired from Arizona State University, caustically examined the economics of these programs in his paper "Notes on the cost of coyote meat in Arizona." Using official reports, Cole determined that governmental expenditures in the 1969 campaign to rid the state of 1,864 coyotes totaled more than 150,000 dollars, or just under 81 dollars per victim. These same reports estimated that coyotes destroyed about eleven hundred domestic animals, about half of which were sheep, although seventeen goats, three dogs and cats, and two horses entered into the tally. Cole wondered out loud whether coyotes could really have been responsible for the deaths of the two horses, but for the purposes of his exercise he accepted the claim that they had. Valuing the three dogs and cats in the account at 14 dollars, Cole calculated the total economic loss laid at the jaws of coyotes at 42,225 dollars.

It does not require a doctorate in economics to guess that the feds would have come out well ahead in 1969 if they had simply paid ranchers the full market value of the animals supposedly killed by coyotes and let it go at that. This conclusion becomes still more attractive if one accepts Cole's calculation that the hundreds of coyotes bagged in 1969 by traps, snares, baited cyanide canisters, hunting dogs and bullets would have dispatched approximately 55,000 jackrabbits, had they been permitted to live to perform this service for the ranchers of Arizona. Because 150 jackrabbits consume enough forage to support one cow or five sheep, the coyote carnage in 1969 cost more than 50,000 dollars in lost cattle production.

In the years since Cole examined the cost of coyote meat, the major government agency responsible for coyote killing has changed from the U.S. Fish and Wildlife Service of the Department of Interior to the Animal Damage Control (ADC) unit of the U.S. Department of Agriculture. The ADC claims that 1,530 Arizona coyotes fell in fiscal year 1987 to leg-hold traps, snares, poison, and even hunters in helicopters and fixed-wing aircraft.

As in 1969, ADC specialists spent a majority of their effort on coyotes, which constituted three-quarters of the total number of

A coyote youngster is about to leap for a snack of tomatillo fruits.

"targeted" individuals taken (excluding birds, jackrabbits and small rodents). If we assume that the hunt for large mammals consumed seventy percent of the nearly half-million-dollar budget of the ADC, then the prorated cost per coyote was more than 215 dollars. Considering inflation, the price tag on coyote meat is probably about what it was nearly twenty years ago.

The ADC report places the value of domestic animals verified to have been dispatched by coyotes at less than 54,000 dollars. Even with the addition of a 150-dollar loss in watermelons, the total bill is still far below the approximately 300,000 dollars devoted to destroying coyotes in 1987.

In states other than Arizona the same relationship between stockmen and coyotes persists. Sheepmen hate coyotes and demand their destruction, despite the fact that nationwide most ranchers lose much less than five percent of their stock to coyotes. Furthermore, biological surveys, which involve direct checking of dead animals, typically put the loss to coyotes at a lower level than that claimed by stockmen.

One result of the enthusiasm for preventing coyotes from satisfying their fondness for sheep (as the bumper sticker says, "Eat Lamb. One Million Coyotes Can't Be Wrong.") has been considerable funding for research on a variety of methods to thwart the wily predator. Some exotic techniques have been developed, including the use of certain breeds of guard dogs that were employed centuries ago to reduce wolf predation in Europe at a time when there were wolves to worry about there. Other still more avant-garde stratagems for countering coyotes include putting out lamb-meat baits laced with lithium chloride, a substance that induces unpleasant vomiting. The idea here is that a few experiences with the drugged meat will turn coyotes against lamb in all forms for good.

A less forgiving method is to place hollow collars filled with a cyanide-based toxin on tethered lambs. In theory, when a confirmed lamb-eater goes for the jugular of one of these attractively vulnerable victims it will puncture the collar, receive a deadly dose of toxin, and expire on the spot. In practice, this does not happen, because the attackers apparently quickly sense that something is amiss and back off before getting a lethal mouthful.

Nor have any other methods proven particularly effective. The ingenuity and tenacity of coyotes are evident in the dimensions of a truly coyote-proof wire fence, which would be at least sixty-six

inches high, topped with a thirty-eight-inch perpendicular over-
hang, and bottomed with a twelve-inch underground apron. The
mesh of the fence would have to be less than six inches by four
inches.

Why are coyotes so devilishly intelligent and so capable of defy-
ing humans? One possibility is that their omnivorous lifestyle has
selected for individuals of above-average intelligence. Animals that
forage for many different kinds of prey items in many different
habitats probably gain a reproductive advantage by investing in
neuronal circuitry that permits them to solve the great diversity of
problems that stand between them and a good meal. Thus, for example, the birds that seem to possess the kind of intelligence that
humans can appreciate (if not approve) are the jays, crows, and
ravens. Many of these species occupy a great range of habitats and
make their livings eating all manner of living things, including some
foods grown by farmers. I note that the ADC had ravens on its hit
list in 1987, dispatching nearly five hundred that had been feasting
on pistachios and apples.

Thanks to the effects of natural selection on the all-purpose
coyote, we need not wax too sentimental about them. They can take
care of themselves. Not only are they able to put their evolved intelligence to use in dealing with the novel problems generated by
canicidal humans, their great reproductive flexibility complements
their behavioral ingenuity. Coyotes, like many other animals, ad-
just their reproductive effort in response to changes in the density
of their local population. In areas where coyotes are scarce, having
been heavily trapped and poisoned, females begin breeding when
they are one year old, and the number of pups that an adult produces averages around eight or nine. In places where humans do
not persecute coyotes, the local population density will be higher
and competition among coyotes greater. Under these conditions,
one-year-old females wait another year before trying to breed, and
the mature females that do reproduce average only three or four
pups. From a population perspective, coyotes compensate for control programs. If many are killed, the survivors simply step up their
reproductive output.

The variation in reproductive rate of young and old females may
seem puzzling if we accept that the evolved goal of coyotes is to
reproduce maximally. But remember that a young coyote vixen that
tries to rear a brood of youngsters in an area filled with older, more

experienced, competing females is likely to fail. She may gain little or nothing for her expensive investment in pups if most die of starvation.

Differences in the lifetime reproductive success of individuals, as measured by the number of surviving descendants each produces, is what drives the evolution of a species. Coyotes are the product of this process and females, therefore, are not inclined to make poor investments in reproductive effort. If conditions are bad, individuals wait or cut back. If the field is open, thanks to human intervention, surviving females quickly fill the void with their progeny, which at least do not have to contend with cold-hearted competitors of their own kind.

In one sense, the hard work of the ADC in Arizona does constitute a kind of success story. The animal controllers have been able to bag about the same number of coyotes year after year, enabling them to justify their existence to a particular constituency. And yet the coyote population has not really been reduced, despite all the refined techniques that humans have dreamed up to apply to this favored "target species." We are a persistent irritant to the coyote world, something that must and will be endured, like the rasping alarms of mobbing cactus wrens and curve-billed thrashers.

A Fur Coat for Summer

You will not be surprised to hear that rock squirrels are much less upsetting to most people than coyotes. For one thing, they are small, about the shape and size of the grey squirrels that live in city parks back East, and so they have small appetites compared to coyotes. For another thing, rock squirrels are confirmed vegetarians; if they should backslide and eat an animal or two, it is likely to be an insect or perhaps a member of their own species. (Although cannibalism has not been reported for rock squirrels, females of a number of other closely related squirrels are known to eat the young of their neighbors.)

Yet another reason Westerners do not get worked up about rock squirrels stems from the little mammal's fondness for rocks, the more the better. Their preferred environment is usually sufficiently hilly and rocky that it is of little economic interest to people, and in many places the squirrels and their homesites have been left alone. In fact, even biologists have more or less ignored this species of ground squirrel, lavishing much more attention on those that live in higher densities in flat, open areas where they can be more easily observed.

The Usery Mountains have some first-class rock piles, and these usually contain resident rock squirrels. The animal is not a secretive creature. Like the much smaller round-tailed ground squirrel of the floodplain, rock squirrels spend a lot of time above ground during the day all summer long, and they are exceptionally noisy. I can easily hear a male rock squirrel calling in his boulder patch a couple hundred meters away down the mountainside. A yelping ground squirrel usually perches on an exposed rock in full view of the desert world and the sun.

The call is a piercing, high-pitched "eek," repeated with great regularity and monotony, as if the animal were just on the verge of producing a somewhat more complex communication but was always frustrated at the last possible moment.

It is the rock squirrel's capacity to endure the summer sunshine so easily that attracted the interest of my colleague Glenn Walsberg, who had previously investigated the same ability in phainopeplas. Rock squirrels, unlike phainopeplas, are not black. Their coats are a salt-and-pepper brown. But under their pale mottled outer coats the squirrels possess a second inner coat, which is black. The outer pelage consists of coarse pale hairs that poke their way through and conceal the much denser and darker layer of fur closer to the skin.

What is the significance of the bilayered pelage of rock squirrels? Their coats are not like the Bedouin's double robe outfit, but they do work together to help the rock squirrel cope with Sonoran Desert temperatures. The outer coat reflects some solar radiation, but its paleness permits much of the energy in sunlight to penetrate to the dark layer. It is at the boundary between the two fur zones that solar radiation is absorbed most strongly. If the inner layer were thin, much of the heat at the boundary layer would reach the skin of the squirrel and raise its body temperature. But the black fur of the rock squirrel is about two-thirds as long as the coarse outer coat. It intercepts incoming heat; because it is dense, it insulates the animal against this heat.

Having established these points using measurements taken from patches of skin and fur removed from sacrificed animals, Walsberg then asked what would happen if one were to vary the ratio of inner to outer coat. Using a mathematical model whose accuracy was confirmed when it accurately predicted the effects of incoming solar radiation on the skin temperature of patches of rock squirrel hide, Walsberg's computer told him that if living squirrels had no inner coats, and thus *relatively* longer outer fur, they would experience a ten-percent gain in heat absorbed from the sun, a substantial and unwanted increase in the summer. On the other hand, if an unusual rock squirrel were to be born without any outer fur it would experience an added fifteen-percent penalty in heat gain.

Squirrels with combination coats are always cooler than animals with monolayered fur, but only one ratio of inner to outer fur yields the minimum heat gain possible. When the inner layer constitutes sixty-seven percent of the outer, rock squirrels are as cool as they are going to be under strong sunlight. Because this ratio matches that actually possessed by rock squirrels, Walsberg concludes that a primary function of the fur structure of the rock squirrel is to help the animal manage solar heat gain in an environment in which there is more than enough solar heat.

Although the ratio of inner to outer coat depths enables rock squirrels to minimize heat gain in the summer, what happens during the winter, when it can get cold in Arizona? The squirrels are active then, too, and keeping heat down is unlikely to be their main thermoregulatory problem. Walsberg and a graduate student, Catherine Schmidt, took a look at how coat structure might affect heat gain during the winter. They collected some rock squirrel specimens in December and January and discovered that the external coat color of these animals was no different from that of squirrels collected in summer. But when they checked the reaction of the coat to solar radiation, Walsberg and Schmidt learned to their amazement and delight that the heat gain through the coat was twenty percent greater than it was for patches of pelage taken from squirrels summering in the Sonoran Desert.

Thus, without changing the appearance of their coats, squirrels do what makes adaptive sense: They reduce heat gain in the broiling summer and permit more heat gain in the cool winter months. They apparently achieve this result by having coats that are thinner in the winter; thinner coats provide less insulation against heat ab-

A rock squirrel on its territorial perch.

sorption than do thicker summer coats. Further, although the hairs in summer and winter coats produce an identical outer appearance, the structure of the hairs and their response to solar radiation changes with the seasons. The effect of the winter changes is to permit solar radiation to penetrate more deeply, thus promoting heat gain at the level of the skin under the coat, a result that can save the animal from having to expend energy to elevate its body temperature on cool days.

Natural selection apparently has achieved the optimal solution to the problem of overheating for rock squirrels in the summer, while not forcing the animal to live with the same super-heat-resistant coat in the winter. Although these animals are unaware of the theoretical beauty of their flexible pelage, they are the beneficiaries of past selection every time they perch comfortably on sunlit rocks in their summer territories and screech out a message of dominion over a land they value more than most humans do.

Hawk Morning

Nothing is moving among the saguaros and palo verdes along the ridgeline, no rock squirrel calls from the stony outcrops on the slopes. The tick-tick of one long-lived creosote grasshopper only accents the stillness of the desert. A three-quarter moon begins to fade in the morning sky.

An antelope ground squirrel breaks the paralysis of the day. It scampers up a gravel patch and under a brittlebush, pulling a large teddy-bear cholla joint that has somehow become attached to its tail. As it slips under a low-lying branch of the brittlebush, the thorny cactus catches on the plant, holding the squirrel prisoner. The little animal scrabbles forward but cannot pull free until, with a final desperate lurch, it breaks away from the barbed spines that bind it to the cholla joint. The sound of its small struggle carries cleanly far across the hard, open hillside.

A red-tailed hawk hangs suspended in the air, barely moving on broad *Buteo* wings. No slipping or tilting like a vulture; steady as she goes. One rigid, flat wing briefly eclipses the moon as the hawk passes overhead. It tucks its wings into its sides and dives down at a slight angle, heading east, picking up speed.

A coyote disrupts the morning with a sudden wild yowling from the wash far below the peaktop. Answering yips come faintly from a canyon miles away. The outburst ends as if the calling coyote had been muzzled in midhowl.

A robberfly buzzes from one bursage to another.

Two kestrels travel on a tangent to the hillside, rising and dipping together, flowing through the air like bits of wood caught in a swirling stream. Above them, two Cooper's hawks float up to the ridge and let the wind carry them to the south briefly before turning to face into the breeze. They drift higher still. The undersides of their wings are a pointillist matrix of dark grey and pure white dots; their long tails are banded and sleek.

The four hawks curl around the flank of Usery Mountain and continue on their migration, heading south across a remnant of lowland desert that yields to a patchwork of houses, trailer parks, and alfalfa fields. The hawks become dots in the blue-grey haze and then disappear on their way to Mexico, swallowed up by the distance and the emptiness of an urban desert.

The Flexible Phainopepla

The trail in McDowell Mountain Park peters out after the first few miles, but the desert is open and the way to the base of the mountains clear. As the plain begins to rise, big boulders lie scrambled on the desert floor. Five Harris's hawks, three flying and two perched, occupy this portion of the park. Their screams reverberate among the rocks, while the birds loop overhead, inspecting part of their communal foraging range.

It is early in the afternoon, and although September is nearly over it still feels like summer. My canteen is empty much sooner than it should be. A wash that drains a portion of the mountains runs toward the east in a broad, sandy avenue through the palo verde and cholla scrub. The fall generation of empress butterflies has emerged, perhaps stimulated by last week's rainstorm, probably the last rain for a long time now that monsoon conditions have ended. Males stand guard at their stations by the hackberries, flickering after anything that might be a passing female.

The hackberries are covered with dark green leaves and little yellow-orange fruits that gleam against their green background. The fruits, half the size of small blueberries, are largely filled with big, inedible seeds, but a thin, palatable coat of sweet flesh around the seed provides a reward for creatures that might disperse the seed. I immediately spit the seeds out after consuming the refreshing fruit, but perhaps Gambel's quail and phainopeplas are more cooperative in carrying seeds throughout the desert.

Covey after covey of quail pop noisily out of thick cover in the wash and rifle away to new hiding places out of the afternoon sun. Flocks of phainopeplas scatter from the hackberries they share with quail. Their breathy, whistled calls, wheep-wheep, float above the explosive wingbeats of the quail. A black-throated grey warbler slips out of the sparse canopy of a palo verde and flies off, staying low on its migratory trail to Mexico.

Phainopeplas are migratory birds too, although they do not follow the traditional north-south pattern by any means. In fact, most phainopeplas leave central Arizona by early May, after breeding in March and April along desert washes and in mesquite bosques. After abandoning the Sonoran Desert the birds scatter to the east, north, and west into cooler and more productive parts of New Mexico, northern Arizona, and California. There they breed again in semi-arid woodlands from May to July before returning to the desert in fall or early winter, in time to feed on hackberries and then mistletoe berries, their staff of life during the winter.

Although there still are details to be uncovered about their migratory pattern, what we know about phainopeplas suggests they are extremely unusual birds. Most North American migrants move between a breeding ground and a nonbreeding, wintering area, but phainopeplas appear to raise one brood in the desert before rearing another family several hundred miles away in adjacent regions. Furthermore, this dual breeding pattern is accompanied by some dramatic changes in the birds' social structure.

In the Sonoran Desert, phainopeplas have all-purpose nesting territories about an acre in size, a plot of land along a wash or in a mesquite forest that contains a rich crop of mistletoe berries. The adult birds depend on this food while they collect insects to feed their brood of two nestlings. A phainopepla pair treats intruders firmly and unpleasantly, driving them away from the resources that will be the basis of both their survival and their reproductive success during the six to eight weeks required to produce a clutch of youngsters in central Arizona.

In California, however, the birds may nest colonially, ten pairs to an acre of riparian woodland rather than one pair to an acre. Each social couple has a mini-territory just large enough to accommodate the tree that holds its nest.

Why the difference in lifestyle in the two regions? One reasonable suggestion is that the resource base that supports adult

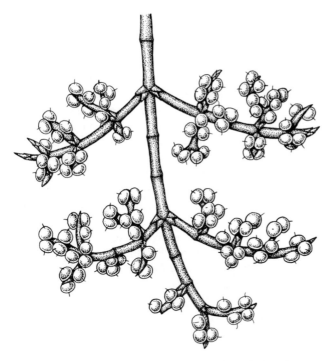

Mistletoe berries sustain the phainopepla through the winter.

phainopeplas differs sharply between desert and temperate woodlands. Instead of dense clumps of desert mistletoe with a berry supply that lasts a pair an average of seven weeks, phainopeplas in
California rely on buckthorn, a shrubby plant that is scattered
more widely than desert mistletoes. More important, the maximum
standing crop on a buckthorn is less than ten percent of the offering
of a mistletoe clump.

Because buckthorns provide less food per individual plant and
because these plants are widely scattered, a phainopepla that attempted to guard this resource against other phainopeplas would
have to defend a very large area indeed to secure as many calories
as would a mistletoe-defender in the Sonoran Desert. The larger
the area, the more costly territoriality becomes, and at some point
the costs will exceed any benefits to be gained from the ven-

ture. Apparently this point is reached during the phainopepla's second breeding season, when they forego large foraging territories altogether.

But why breed in loose colonies? There are any number of untested hypotheses to account for the sociality of phainopeplas summering in California, including the possibility that the birds gather together in order to take advantage of each other's food finds. The birds do occasionally follow departing neighbors to a fruiting buckthorn whose location might have been unknown to them. And when one bird finds a swarm of flies or other insects in the evening, others living nearby can see the hunter at work and are quick to join him or her at the productive foraging site. Living with others probably facilitates social flycatching and so may provide a caloric bonus for the birds that choose to nest in sight of their Californian neighbors; in Arizona, neighbors would only represent a drain on the banks of mistletoe berries clustered within a territory.

The social flexibility of phainopeplas provides additional evidence that sociality is a trait whose reproductive value depends on any number of things. Under one set of conditions phainopeplas are decidedly antisocial, except to their mates, with whom they defend a large feeding territory. Under other conditions the birds are far more tolerant of others and may even engage in a number of communal activities, such as flycatching.

One of the great insights that has come from rigorously thinking about the costs and benefits of traits to individuals, as measured by their impact on individual reproductive success, has been to escape from the notion that there is some sort of absolute scale of characteristics in the animal kingdom, running from primitive, inferior, and second rate to advanced, superior, and first rate. The phainopeplas show us that sociality's value is measured in the currency of individual reproductive success, and that even within a potentially social species there may be a profitable time to go it alone.

Today, with the next Arizona breeding season many months away, the phainopeplas have formed foraging flocks, perhaps to enjoy safety in numbers in a world where yellow-eyed Cooper's hawks dart through the thickets of vegetation along washes. A pod of phainopeplas, black males and grey females, springs out of an ironwood and scatters in all directions, white wing patches flashing collectively like a fistful of oversized confetti thrown into the desert sky.

The Fall of Summer

The desert plain slopes gently toward the recumbent saguaro giant. It is a deliciously cool morning after a night in which the temperature in town dropped to the high 60s. By early morning, all through the urban megalopolis of Greater Phoenix, people have opened their windows to encourage the refreshing night air to enter their houses. The stale, refrigerated air seemed reluctant to yield its dominion indoors at our place, but here in the desert the atmosphere is radiant, clean, and — best of all — naturally cool. Perhaps the five-month summer has finally been broken.

The trash by the desert track drops behind as the trail moves away from the areas frequented by people. A cactus wren perches atop a standing saguaro, as if to survey a glorious new world. There is a relaxation of tension in the desert, an easing by two or three notches in the sensation of encirclement by heat, by pavement, by people. It feels good. It feels like fall.

The jumbled mounds of woodrats provide cairns that mark the trail. Each animal has pulled together a ratbag collection of blackened sticks from ironwoods in the wash, dried rinds of saguaro fruits, prickly pear cactus pads, and cholla cactus joints. One mound contains a crushed aluminum beer can, another a portion of a plastic milk bottle.

A vegetarian coyote's scat lies on the ground, full of the seeds of buffalo gourd. Nearby, fragile brown tubes encase a cluster of dead globe mallow stems. Tiny desert termites have constructed these delicate extensions of their underground tunnels, mud pellet by mud pellet. In the darkness of their tubes the almost transparent termite workers strip the plant fibers from the mallow stems and transport them down into the safety of their nest chambers. There the dried plant materials will be digested and recycled, ultimately to advance the reproductive success of the workers' parents, a fertile queen and king that never willingly see the light of day. After the worker termites have finished eating the plant stems they have encased in mud, the hollow tubes stand briefly on their own before crumbling when the wind comes to shake them down.

The fallen saguaro is much more enduring than the termite tubes that poke up into mallows and coat dead twigs lying on the desert, but even the saguaro has aged considerably since the stormy day when its life ended. Today its body holds no remaining hint of succulence. The interlocked ribs that supported the main trunk are smooth and tan, sun-polished, heat-cured. No insect wanders over the vastly diminished surface of the saguaro in search of food or mates. The delicate, pencil-thin ribs of a young arm lie pressed flat on desert gravel, a mere suggestion of what once was a three-dimensional structure. Under the heat of months past the little ribs have bent and curled into commas, quotation marks, parentheses, and flourishes — as if the saguaro has been writing its own epitaph during the Sonoran Desert summer.

References

MAY

The Fall and Decline of a Giant

Barker, J. S. F., and W. T. Starmer (eds.). 1982. *Ecological Genetics and Evolution: The Cactus-Yeast-Drosophila Model System*. Sydney, Academic Press.

Mangan, R. L. 1979. Reproductive behavior of the cactus fly, *Odontoloxozus longicornis*, male territoriality and female guarding as adaptive strategies. *Behavioral Ecology and Sociobiology* 4:265−78.

Markow, T. A. 1988. Reproductive behavior of *Drosophila melanogaster* and *Drosophila nigrospiracula* in the field and in the laboratory. *Journal of Comparative Psychology* 2:169−73.

Myles, T. G. 1986. Oviposition and development of *Volucella isabellina* (Diptera: Syrphidae) on saguaro cactus, *Cereus giganteus*. *Entomological News* 97:104−08.

Black Plumage — Desert Heat

Shkolnik, A., C. R. Tayler, V. Finch, and A. Borut. 1980. Why do Bedouins wear black robes in hot deserts? *Nature* 283:373−75.

Walsberg, G. E. 1982. Coat color, solar heat gain, and conspicuousness in the phainopepla. *Auk* 99:495−502.

———. 1983. Coat color and solar heat gain in animals. *BioScience* 33:88−91.

Goatsucker Myths?

Jackson, H. O. 1985. Commentary and observations on the alleged transportation of eggs and young by caprimulgids. *Wilson Bulletin* 97:381−85.

Phillips, A. R., J. Marshall, and G. Monson. 1964. *The Birds of Arizona*. Tucson, University of Arizona Press.

Empress Butterflies: Hooked on Hackberry

Rutowski, R. L., and G. W. Gilchrist. 1988. Male mate-locating behavior in the empress butterfly, *Asterocampa leilia* (Nymphalidae). *Journal of Research on the Lepidoptera* 26:1−12.

Broom-rapes, Cancer-roots, and Strangle-vetches

Kuijt, J. 1969. *The Biology of Parasitic Flowering Plants*. Berkeley, University of California Press.

Musselman, L. J. 1980. The biology of *Striga, Orobanche* and other root-parasitic weeds. *Annual Reviews of Phytology* 18:463–89.

Freedom Fighters

Alcock, J. 1984. Long-term maintenance of size variation in populations of *Centris pallida* (Hymenoptera: Anthophoridae). *Evolution* 38:220–23.

Alcock, J., and S. L. Buchmann. 1985. The significance of the post-insemination display of male *Centris pallida* (Hymenoptera: Anthophoridae). *Zeitschrift für Tierpsychologie*, 68:231–43.

———. 1976. Location before emergence of the female bee, *Centris pallida*, by its male (Hymenoptera: Anthophoridae). *Journal of Zoology* 179:189–99.

Alcock, J., C. E. Jones, and S. L. Buchmann. 1976. The nesting behavior of three species of *Centris* (Hymenoptera: Anthophoridae). *Journal of the Kansas Entomological Society* 49:469–74.

———. 1977. Male mating strategies in the bee *Centris pallida* Fox (Hymenoptera: Anthophoridae). *American Naturalist* 111:145–55.

Hands Off the Gila Monster!

Porzer, L. M. 1981. Movement, behavior, and body temperature of the gila monster (*Heloderma suspectum*) in Queen Creek, Pinal County, Arizona. Unpublished master's thesis, Arizona State University.

Smith, R. L. 1982. *Venomous Animals of Arizona*. Tucson, University of Arizona Cooperative Extension Service.

JUNE

Poorwill

Harrison, C. 1978. *A Field Guide to the Nests, Eggs and Nestlings of North American Birds*. Glasgow, Collins.

Jaeger, E. C. 1949. Further observations on the hibernation of the poor-will. *Condor* 51:105–09.

How to Wave to a Predator — and Get Away with It

Hasson, O., R. Hibbard, and G. Ceballos. 1989. The pursuit deterrent function of tail-wagging in the zebra-tailed lizard (*Callisaurus draconoides*). *Canadian Journal of Zoology* 67:1203–09.

Smythe, N. 1970. On the existence of "pursuit invitation" signals in mammals. *American Naturalist* 104:491–94.

Williams, G. C. 1966. *Adaptation and Natural Selection*. Princeton, Princeton University Press.

Wittenberger, J. F. 1981. *Animal Social Behavior*. Boston, Duxbury Press.

Wynne-Edwards, V. C. 1962. *Animal Dispersion in Relation to Social Behaviour*. Edinburgh, Oliver & Boyd.

Altruism Among Ground Squirrels

Dunford, C. 1977. Kin selection for ground squirrel alarm calls. *American Naturalist* 111:782–85.
———. 1977. Social system of round-tailed ground squirrels. *Animal Behaviour* 25:885–906.
Murie, J. O., and G. R. Michener (eds.). 1984. *The Biology of Ground-Dwelling Squirrels: Annual Cycles, Behavioral Ecology, and Sociality*. Lincoln, University of Nebraska Press.
Sherman, P. 1977. Nepotism and the evolution of alarm calls. *Science* 197:1246–53.

Range Wars

Ewald, P. W. 1985. Influence of asymmetries in resource quality and age on aggression and dominance in black-chinned hummingbirds. *Animal Behaviour* 33:705–19.
Ewald, P. W., and R. J. Bransfield. 1987. Territory quality and territorial behavior in two sympatric species of hummingbirds. *Behavioral Ecology and Sociobiology* 20:285–93.

The Hard Lives and Hard Times of Brittlebush

Schulze, E. D., R. H. Robichaux, J. Grace, P. W. Rundel, and J. R. Ehrlinger. 1987. Plant water balance. *BioScience* 37:30–37.

Burn, Desert, Burn

Cave, G. H., and D. T. Patten. 1984. Short-term vegetation responses to fire in the upper Sonoran Desert. *Journal of Range Management* 37:491–96.
Loftin, S. R. 1987. Postfire dynamics of a Sonoran Desert ecosystem. Unpublished master's thesis, Arizona State University.
Patten, D. T., and G. H. Cave. 1984. Fire temperatures and physical characteristics of a controlled burn in the upper Sonoran Desert. *Journal of Range Management* 37:277–80.

The Usery Mountain Mobbers

Curio, E. 1978. The adaptive significance of avian mobbing. I: Teleonomic hypotheses and predictions. *Zeitschrift für Tierpsychologie* 48:175–83.
Curio, E., U. Ernst, and W. Vieth. 1978. The adaptive significance of avian mobbing. II: Cultural transmission of enemy recognition in blackbirds: Effectiveness and some constraints. *Zeitschrift für Tierpsychologie* 48:184–202.

JULY

How to Win Mates and Influence Enemies

Goldsmith, S. K. 1987. The mating system and alternative reproductive behaviors of *Dendrobias mandibularis* (Coleoptera: Cerambycidae). *Behavioral Ecology and Sociobiology* 20:111–15.

————. 1987. Resource distribution and its effect on the mating system of a longhorned beetle, *Perarthrus linsleyi* (Coleoptera: Cerambycidae). *Oecologia* 73:317–20.

Pleasant Memories

Bureau of Reclamation. 1976. *Environmental Impact Statement: Orme Dam and Reservoir, Central Arizona Project, Arizona — New Mexico.*

Greenfield, M. D., T. E. Shelly, and K. R. Downum. 1987. Variation in host plant quality: Implications for territoriality in a desert grasshopper. *Ecology* 68:828–38.

Otte, D., and A. Joern. 1975. Insect territoriality and its evolution: Population studies of desert grasshoppers on creosote bushes. *Journal of Animal Ecology* 44:29–54.

Shelly, T. E., M. D. Greenfield, and K. R. Downum. 1987. Variation in host plant quality: Influences on the mating system of a desert grasshopper. *Animal Behaviour* 35:1200–09.

Cooperative Killers and Lovers

Bednarz, J. C. 1988. Cooperative hunting in Harris' hawks (*Parabuteo unicinctus*). *Science* 239:1525–27.

Brown, J. L. 1987. *Helping and Communal Breeding in Birds.* Princeton, Princeton University Press.

Of Leks and Carpenter Bees

Alcock, J., and A. P. Smith. 1987. Leks, hilltopping and female choice in the carpenter bee *Xylocopa* (*Neoxylocopa*) *varipuncta*. *Journal of Zoology* 211:1–10.

Andersen, J. F., S. L. Buchmann, D. Weisleder, R. D. Plattner, and R. L. Minckley. 1987. Identification of thoracic gland constituents from male *Xylocopa* spp. Latreille (Hymenoptera: Anthophoridae) from Arizona. *Journal of Chemical Ecology* 14:1153–62.

Marshall, L.D., and J. Alcock. 1981. The evolution of the mating system of the carpenter bee *Xylocopa varipuncta* (Hymenoptera: Anthophoridae). *Journal of Zoology*, 193:315–24.

All Used Up

Cordell, L. 1984. *Prehistory of the Southwest.* New York, Academic Press.

Doyel, D. E. 1979. The prehistoric Hohokam of the Arizona desert. *American Scientist* 67:544–54.

Masse, B. 1981. Prehistoric irrigation systems in the Salt River Valley, Arizona. *Science* 214:408–15.

Mimics, Aggressive and Otherwise

Cole, F. R. 1969. *The Flies of Western North America*. Berkeley, University of California Press.

Linsley, E. G. 1970. Ethology of some bee- and wasp-killing robber flies of southeastern Arizona and western New Mexico. *University of California Publications in Entomology* 16:357–92.

Poulton, E. B. 1904. The mimicry of Aculeata by the Asilidae and *Volucella*, and its probable significance. *Transactions of the Entomological Society of London*, 1904:661–65.

Waldbauer, G. P., J. G. Sternburg, and C. T. Maier. 1979. Phenological relationship of wasps, bumblebees, their mimics, and insectivorous birds in an Illinois sand area. *Ecology* 58:583–91.

Wilcox, J., and N. Papavero. 1971. The American genera of Mydidae (Diptera), with the description of three new genera and two new species. *Arquivos de Zoologia* (Sao Paulo) 21:41–119.

AUGUST

Flying in the Rain

Hölldobler, B. 1976. The behavioral ecology of mating in harvester ants (Hymenoptera: Formicidae: *Pogonomyrmex*). *Behavioral Ecology and Sociobiology* 1:405–23.

The Seasons of the Peccary

Parker, G. A., and R. G. Pearson. 1976. Possible origin and adaptive significance of mounting behaviour shown by some female mammals in estrus. *Journal of Natural History* 10:241–45.

Sowls, L. K. 1984. *The Peccaries*. Tucson, University of Arizona Press.

August's Saguaro

McAuliffe, J. R. 1984. Sahuaro-nurse tree associations in the Sonoran Desert: Competitive effects of sahuaros. *Oecologia* 64:319–21.

McAuliffe, J. R., and P. Hendricks. 1988. Determinants of the vertical distributions of woodpecker nest cavities in the sahuaro cactus. *Condor* 90:791–801.

A Wolf in Vulture's Clothing

Mueller, H. C. 1972. Zone-tailed hawk and turkey vulture: Mimicry or aerodynamics? *Condor* 74:221–22.

Willis, E. O. 1963. Is the zone-tailed hawk a mimic of the turkey vulture? *Condor* 65:313–17.

Carotenoids Make the Man

Crews, D. 1975. Effects of different components of male courtship behaviour on environmentally induced ovarian recrudescence and mating preferences in the lizard, *Anolis carolinensis*. *Animal Behaviour* 23:349–56.

Kodric-Brown, A. 1985. Female preference and sexual selection for male coloration in the guppy (*Poecilia reticulata*). *Behavioral Ecology and Sociobiology* 17:199–206.

Kodric-Brown, A., and J. H. Brown. 1984. Truth in advertising: The kinds of traits favored by sexual selection. *American Naturalist* 124:309–23.

Sigmund, W. R. 1983. Female preference for *Anolis carolinensis* males as a function of dewlap color and background coloration. *Journal of Herpetology* 17:137–43.

A Recommendation for Scorpions

Birkhead, T. R., K. E. Lee, and P. Young. 1988. Sexual cannibalism in the praying mantis *Hierodula membranacea*. *Behaviour* 106:112–18.

Buskirk, R. E., C. Frolich, and K. G. Ross. 1984. The natural selection of sexual cannibalism. *American Naturalist* 123:612–25.

Hadley, N. F. 1988. Environmental physiology. In *Biology of Scorpions*, edited by G. A. Polis. Palo Alto, Stanford University Press.

Liske, E., and W. J. Davis. 1986. Courtship and mating behaviour of the Chinese praying mantis, *Tenodera aridifolia sinensis*. *Animal Behaviour* 35:1524–37.

Meffe, G. K., and M. L. Crump. 1987. Possible growth and reproductive benefits of cannibalism in the mosquitofish. *American Naturalist* 129:203–12.

Polis, G. A. 1981. The evolution and dynamics of intraspecific predation. *Annual Review of Ecology Systematics* 12:225–51.

———. (ed.). 1988. *Biology of Scorpions*. Palo Alto, Stanford University Press.

Polis, G. A., and S. J. McCormick. 1987. Intraguild predation and competition among desert scorpions. *Ecology* 68:332–43.

SEPTEMBER

The Cost of Coyote Meat: An Update

Bekoff, M. (ed.). 1978. *Coyotes: Biology, Behavior and Management.* New York, Academic Press.

Cole, G. A. 1970. Notes on the cost of coyote meat in Arizona. *Journal of Arizona Academy of Science* 6:2; 85.

A Fur Coat for Summer

Walsberg, G. E. 1988. The significance of coat structure for solar heat gain in the rock squirrel, *Spermophilus variegatus*. *Journal of Experimental Biology* 138:243–57.

Walsberg, G. E., and C. A. Schmidt. 1989. Seasonal adjustment of solar heat gain in a desert mammal by altering coat properties independent of surface coloration. *Journal of Experimental Biology* 142:387–400.

The Flexible Phainopepla

Walsberg, G. E. 1977. Ecology and energetics of contrasting social systems in *Phainopepla nitens* (Aves: Ptilogonatidae). *University of California Publications in Zoology*, 108:1–63.

———. 1978. Brood size and the use of time and energy by the phainopepla. *Ecology* 59:147–53.

Index

ABOUT THE AUTHOR

John Alcock is Regent's Professor of Zoology at Arizona State University and the author of *Animal Behavior: An Evolutionary Approach*, the most widely used textbook in animal behavior. For much of his career he has studied insect behavior in the Sonoran Desert of central Arizona, where he has developed a great admiration for the desert and its natural inhabitants. Alcock has conveyed his enthusiasm for desert biology to the reading public in magazine articles for *Natural History* and *Arizona Highways* and in the books *Sonoran Desert Spring* and *The Kookaburras' Song*, the latter published by The University of Arizona Press in 1988.